THE UNIVERSE IS YOUR SEARCH ENGINE

A User's Guide to the Science of Attraction

ANITA M. SCOTT

BALBOA.PRESS
A DIVISION OF HAY HOUSE

Balboa Press books may be ordered through booksellers or by contacting:

Balboa Press
A Division of Hay House
1663 Liberty Drive
Bloomington, IN 47403
www.balboapress.com
1 (877) 407-4847

Because of the dynamic nature of the Internet, any web addresses or links contained in this book may have changed since publication and may no longer be valid. The views expressed in this work are solely those of the author and do not necessarily reflect the views of the publisher, and the publisher hereby disclaims any responsibility for them.

The author of this book does not dispense medical advice or prescribe the use of any technique as a form of treatment for physical, emotional, or medical problems without the advice of a physician, either directly or indirectly. The intent of the author is only to offer information of a general nature to help you in your quest for emotional and spiritual well-being. In the event you use any of the information in this book for yourself, which is your constitutional right, the author and the publisher assume no responsibility for your actions.

Any people depicted in stock imagery provided by Getty Images are models, and such images are being used for illustrative purposes only.
Certain stock imagery © Getty Images.

Print information available on the last page.

ISBN: 978-1-9822-4006-6 (sc)
ISBN: 978-1-9822-4008-0 (hc)
ISBN: 978-1-9822-4007-3 (e)

Library of Congress Control Number: 2019920691

Balboa Press rev. date: 06/01/2020

DEDICATION

I dedicate this book to my beautiful grandchildren, Tegan and Jordan. My greatest wish for them is that they grow up with a full understanding and mastery of the Universe's Search Engine to create and live the life of their most fantastical dreams (with me as their role model)!

Acknowledgements

I've been on a journey of learning and teaching universal principles for more than a decade with my first workshop held in 2008. Many friends and family members have been with me throughout, allowing me to test theories, participating in case studies, and helping with reviews of countless iterations of content.

I acknowledge each of you for your support along the path that has led to the publication of this book. You've been an instrumental part of my work and your hand is included in uplifting and improving the lives of many. Thank you!

If you can bear it, I'm looking forward to more decades of the same!

John Scott
Skye Scott
Sterling Scott
Asami Samples
Grayson Samples
Johanna Kapka
Wendy Pettus
Cari Jaquet
Lili Jaquet
Jacqueline Scott
William H. Holtkamp
E.J. Youngblood
Jim Johnson

Dana Look-Arimoto
Leah Davis
Sharon Beloli
Sue Yeager
Valerie Morignat, PhD
Dawn Stansfield
Wenonah Hoye
Jill Wesley
Scott Richmond
Ann-Marie Nieves
Kelly Notaras
Sheila Scott

PRAISE FOR
THE UNIVERSE IS YOUR SEARCH ENGINE

"This book changed my life and re-nourished my soul! I've read dozens of spirituality books and not one of them combines the science with practical application in such a simple form. It's at the same level as Deepak Chopra and Oprah."
—E.J. Youngblood, Elyjah Tribe Founder

*"**THE UNIVERSE IS YOUR SEARCH ENGINE** is my bible. It changed the way I see everything, then everything changed!"*
—Asami Yamada-Samples, Founder of Yamada Photography Hawaii

"Each time I read your book I get more amazed at its potential to change lives. You have categorically explained and defined the science behind positive thinking. Bravo!"
—Dannie Jackson, Instructional Designer

"Anita has unlocked the key that so many of us have been yearning for yet struggled with. Thank you for simplifying the intangible. Understanding how the universe actually works for us and adopting the lessons will change readers lives instantly."
—Dana Look-Arimoto, Author, Speaker, Coach, Phoenix 5 Founder

"Thank you for writing this book that has the power to awaken and uplift others. I love that it's a practical approach to having conscious and deliberate interactions with what otherwise is a system designed to trigger automatic responses. This book is very powerful and written with a genuine voice. It's a delightful guide to a more deliberate and meaningful life."
—Valerie Morignat, Ph.D., Founder and CEO of Intelligent Story

CONTENTS

PREFACE

As magnificent creators we each have a controller in the palm of our hand, yet very few are aware of the incredible powers at our fingertips and even fewer take ownership and harness that power. But that's all about to change!

The universal laws of science, quantum physics, and metaphysics are what bring about the entirety of your life experience across the good, bad, or ugly. Some of the universal forces captured herein were pondered and written about centuries ago by truly great minds the likes of Nikola Tesla, Albert Einstein, Henry Ford, Napoleon Hill, and Thomas Edison. As visionaries they had one thing in common. They understood many of these principles (presented to you in this book!) and wielded them to bring about their innovations and successes. Knowing the power to vastly improve people's lives, they did their best to share this information, yet adoption failed to gain traction with the masses. Why?

Several deterrents impeded adoption. First, only within the last century have many principles been scientifically proven—until then, they were theoretical and therefore not taken seriously (seen as hippie and before that witchery). Second, the inner workings of the Universe are multifaceted and can prove challenging to comprehend. Third, their invisibility compounds the struggle to conceptualize how they impact you directly. Fourth, some resist putting in the effort needed to harness these universal laws. Last, the platforms and speed with which information is disseminated today were not available.

Combined, these elements precluded generating enough momentum to propel this life changing information into the mainstream.

In the twenty-first century, however, we are on the precipice of human evolution! While the invisibility and level of effort remain, as we've moved through time the other deterrents have fallen by the wayside. With scientific proof and the proliferation of information circulating at lightning speed, a sea change is brewing. This book unlocks and deciphers principles across science, quantum physics, and metaphysics like never before, with complex concepts served up in digestible, bite-size pieces so they're easy for anyone to comprehend and apply.

The Universe Is Your Search Engine also cracks the code on the Law of Attraction in purely scientific terms, so while few today are deliberate creators, more and more people are learning, accessing, and mastering these superpowers (in the plural) to live their very best life.

My favorite quote from Mahatma Gandhi is, "Be the change that you wish to see in the world." In service of my passion to help others, my hope for readers is that they come away with a firm understanding of what the Universe's Search Engine is, how it works, and how to harness its power to dramatically improve their quality of life. This book is my dare to change the world.

SUGGESTIONS TO MY READERS

The chapters in this book are engineered to build off of one another. Each propels your understanding of the Universe's Search Engine and other universal principles—what they are, how they work, and how to harness their power—to live your best life whether that means a total transformation or just an upgrade. Chapter by chapter momentum grows, and your evolution crescendos into the master creator you were born to be, with the ability to create your future reality!

This book is organized into three parts:

- **Part 1: The Law of Attraction Is The Universe's Search Engine**
  Deciphers the science behind the Universe's Search Engine and delves into how to harness its power.
- **Part 2: Other Components**
  Presents other important components influencing your life experience so you can actively harness all avenues.
- **Part 3: Workbook**
  Provides exercises and challenges to support principle application that facilitates and expedites improvements.

To make full use of this book I recommend you read the chapters in chronological order, completing the exercises as they appear so by the time you finish you'll have already begun experiencing improvements.

Once you've completed the book, I suggest you slowly reread and redo the exercises in depth. With each reading your understanding deepens along with your ability to master the principles.

Now, get ready to be taken on a thrilling journey through amazing scientific discoveries with mind-blowing twists and turns. By the end, you'll be exhilarated by the infinite potentiality of how the rest of your life unfolds, with the controller squarely in your hands. Buckle up and enjoy the (r)evolutionary ride!

PART I:
THE LAW OF ATTRACTION
IS THE UNIVERSE'S
SEARCH ENGINE

This section systematically explains the science responsible for the Law of Attraction as the Universe's Search Engine. What it is, how it works, and the many ways to actively harness its power.

CHAPTER 1
SCIENCE MATTERS

"The good thing about science is that it's true
whether or not you believe in it."
–Neil DeGrasse Tyson

Search Engine: *noun*
A search engine is a service that allows Internet users to search for content via the World Wide Web (WWW). A user enters keywords or key phrases into a search engine and receives a list of Web content results in the form of websites, images, videos or other online data (Techopedia).

You may already be familiar with search engines like Google, Bing, and Yahoo. In layman's terms, a search engine is a software program designed to quickly find and return matches to what you're searching for on the Internet. This software acts like a filter that sits on top of the World Wide Web screening everything that's out there so you don't have to drudge through it all. You simply enter keywords or phrases to narrow down your search, and presto Google takes less than a second to deliver results.

Whittled down to the simplest of descriptions a search engine a) picks up keywords, b) searches for, and c) returns content matches.

The Universe's Search Engine

What if I told you that the Universe has its own search engine, that functions like Google, except it uses your *thoughts* instead of keywords? And, in place of content, the Universe's Search Engine *returns real-life experiences.*

If a technology like this existed, would you be interested in knowing how it works? A better question is: Would you want to learn how to use and harness its power to return the life of your dreams?

The truth of the matter is this technology has been available since the beginning of time. Even more fascinating, you've been using it unknowingly throughout your entire lifetime. In fact, it's responsible for the life you have today.

THIS TECHNOLOGY ISN'T A SECRET—*ITS SCIENCE!*

Part I of this book deciphers the science behind the Universe's Search Engine, decoding exactly how thoughts replace keywords, and how real-life experiences are returned instead of content.

Becoming a Deliberate Creator

Once you know how the Universe's Search Engine works and plug in to harness its power as a deliberate creator, there's nothing stopping you from living your very best life. By "deliberate creator" I mean that you intentionally create your future reality by leveraging the Universe's Search Engine to control the life experiences returned across health, wealth, love, peace, and anything else that brings you unbridled joy. Whether this means upgrading a few aspects of your life or a complete transformation, both are entirely possible and completely up to you.

Setting the Framework

Since the end-to-end functionality of the Universe's Search Engine is rooted in science, comprehending precisely what it is and how it works requires understanding a few science fundamentals, which for the sake of simplicity I have divided into four "pillars."

Fair warning: Once you learn these scientific principles, you can't put the toothpaste back in the tube, so to speak. This information will change the way you see, experience, and approach life forevermore.

Pillar 1: Elementary Science 101 Refresher

This first pillar is composed of basic science terms and definitions you may remember learning in elementary school or junior high:

a) **Matter**: Everything with physical substance.
b) **Atoms**: The basic building blocks of matter, made up of pure energy in the form of subatomic particles.
c) **Vibrations**: Those subatomic particles constantly explode with energy creating vibrations.
d) **Motion**: Those vibrations produce a constant state of motion.

Therefore, while matter looks solid to the human eye—think of a table or rock—it's actually in a constant state of motion, vibrating with pure energy (figure 1).

Figure 1: Subatomic particles produce vibrations creating a constant state of vibration.

Pillar 2: Electromagnetic Waves

Those continuous vibrations produce the second pillar, *electromagnetic waves*, which are made up of two components:

1) **Wavelength**: The wave's *length,* or distance between two peaks or valleys (figure 2).

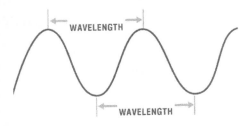

Figure 2: A wavelength is the distance between a wave's peaks and valleys.

2) **Frequency**: How *frequently* a wavelength completes a cycle of motion per second (figure 3).

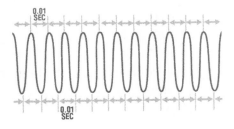

Figure 3: Frequency is how many waves occur per second.

Frequencies range from high to low. High frequencies have shorter intervals with waves closer together (figure 4), and low frequencies have intervals with waves spread farther apart (figure 5).

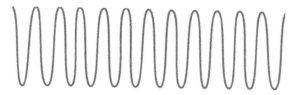

Figure 4: Quicker intervals produce higher frequencies.

Figure 5: Slower intervals produce lower frequencies.

Those emitted frequencies contain information and cascade away from matter, similar to how a pebble dropped into water creates ripples that move outwards (figure 6).

Figure 6: Vibrations create electromagnetic waves that emit information outwards.

With an understanding of how vibrational frequencies constantly emit information away from matter, we move to the next pillar.

Pillar 3: Frequency Highway

The third pillar is the energy field similar to, if not the same as, the field that enables all wireless technology to work. It's what we call the *frequency highway* because it's the conduit that brings together matching frequencies. This highway is available across the entire planet (figure 7).

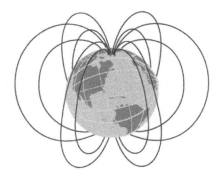

Figure 7: The frequency highway encapsulates the globe.

Because it's invisible you may not be aware of its presence, but this highway is incredibly prominent in your everyday life. The most commonly known use is music playing on the radio. Here's how that works:

1. Radio stations package up a song's data elements by converting music into radio frequency (RF) waves.
2. Once emitted, that information is carried by the frequency highway *in search of a frequency match.*
3. Radio antennas are programmed to receive specific frequencies, so when a frequency match is found the data elements reassemble to *return an experience* via the radio playing the song.

With no wires attached you can hear music, and by tuning into different frequencies (changing lanes) you have a multitude of listening options.

There are infinite lanes on the frequency highway—think of it as a super highway where each lane carries a particular frequency to a distinct destination. There are lanes that enable keyless entry into cars, other lanes for changing channels on televisions, others for texting, video doorbells, cell phones, and thousands more. Once the chosen frequency arrives at the matching frequency destination, an experience is instantaneously returned.

We rely heavily on this super highway to provide numerous experiences on a daily basis.

Pillar 4: HEAR THIS – The Frequency Highway Is the Universe's Search Engine

I digress momentarily to explain what to expect when you come across a "HEAR THIS" subhead. When Sterling, my youngest son, was a toddler his way of getting our attention was to demand, "Hear this!" My husband and I thought it was cute so to this day we use it when we get excited about sharing new concepts with each other.

So HEAR THIS: The frequency highway is the Universe's Search Engine because it functions like Google a) picking up, b) searching for, and c) returning matches. Here's what this looks like side-by-side:

GOOGLE	FREQUENCY HIGHWAY
a) Picks up: Keywords & phrases	a) Picks up: Emitted frequencies
b) Searches for: Keyword matches	b) Searches for: Frequency matches
c) Returns: Content	c) Returns: Experiences

To illustrate how the frequency highway mirrors Google's functionality, take the example of using a remote control to open your garage door. When clicked the remote emits a signal (aka information) and the frequency highway picks it up, and searches for a frequency match. When a signal match is located an experience occurs in the form of your garage door opening.

That same remote won't open your neighbor's garage or turn your television on because there's no frequency match. There must be a frequency match between *both* for an experience to occur.

The concept of the frequency highway being the Universe's Search Engine, functioning like Google by a) picking up, b) searching for vibratory frequency matches, and c) returning results in the form of *experiences* is the fourth and final pillar.

Universe's *Vs.* Universal Search Engine

You can call the frequency highway the *Universe's* Search Engine or the *Universal* Search Engine because both terms apply. This functionality is woven into the fabric of our cosmos, and is accessible to everyone at all times.

The scientific principles covered within these four pillars apply to all matter, inanimate or not, and carry through as the foundation for all that comes next.

Key Principles

1. Pillar 1: Basic science
    a. All matter is comprised of atoms.
    b. Atoms are pure energy in a constant state of vibration.
    c. Vibrations produce wavelengths and frequencies.
    d. Wavelengths and vibrational frequencies create electromagnetic waves.
    e. High frequencies have waves with quicker intervals.
    f. Low frequencies have waves with slower intervals.

2. Pillar 2: Electromagnetic waves contain information specific to the matter exuding it.
3. Pillar 3: The frequency highway is pervasive and encompasses the globe.
4. Pillar 4: The frequency highway is the Universe's Search Engine, functioning like a browser by searching for and returning matches.
5. These principles apply to all matter, inanimate or not.

CHAPTER 2
ENERGY MATTERS

*"If you want to find the secrets of the Universe, think
in terms of energy, frequency and vibration."*
–Nikola Tesla

Now that you know the frequency highway is the Universe's
Search Engine we will delve into understanding more about how it
works, overlaying the four pillars of science covered in the first chapter
with emissions responsible for returning *your* life experiences.

You Are Pure Energy

If inanimate objects are constantly producing and emitting
information, consider what's being exuded from living things such
as plants, animals, and mammals—including you!

You're alive on this Earth thanks to the energy coursing throughout
your body, and you enjoy life in large part through your senses that
come to you as electrical impulses.

To showcase this, let's sharpen the lens on your sense of hearing.
When someone speaks their voice produces *sound waves* that the
Universe's Search Engine a) *picks up* in b) *search of a frequency
match*. In this case, ears, where sound waves convert into electrical
impulses that are processed and decoded by the brain to c) *return the
experience* of hearing.

Dog whistles also produce sound waves, but their frequency is much higher and therefore out of range for human ears. While there's an experience for dogs, there isn't one for you because it's not on a lane that can reach you—there is no vibratory frequency *match*.

Though pertinent, the quality of your life is not dictated or formed by the energy flowing through your body, the electrical impulses that enable your five senses, or even the physical energy exerted when you wash a car, work out, or raise a family.

Introduction: *Thoughts*

The energy most involved in creating your life experiences comes from your very own thoughts.

How can that be?

Each thought you have produces electrical impulses that spark neurons. Those firing neurons produce electromagnetic waves that emit vibrational frequencies outward, just like matter emitting information (figure 8).[1] The difference is, electromagnetic waves produced by firing neurons have distinctive vibrational frequencies ranging from high to low according to what you are thinking about.

Figure 8: Firing neurons emit electromagnetic waves known as "thoughts."

Vibratory Frequency Ranges

Positive thoughts about love, appreciation, joy, and more produce and emit *high frequency vibrations* (figure 9).

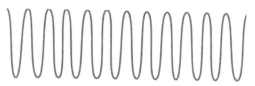

Figure 9: Imaginary sample of positive thoughts producing wavelengths with higher frequencies.

You can tell when you're emitting high frequency vibes because you feel lighter, more empowered, and experience greater clarity—it feels like you're in the zone and everything's going your way.

Negative thoughts like jealousy, revenge, or hate are the opposite polarity and emanate low frequencies with waves spread further apart. Negative frequencies make your energy denser, which is why problems feel heavy, and why it takes a lot more effort to do anything. It feels as though you're moving through quicksand (figure 10).

Figure 10: Imaginary sample of negative thoughts producing wavelengths with lower frequencies.

One Thought at a Time

On average you have 60,000 to 80,000 thoughts per day. This equates to a new thought every 1.2 seconds.[2] If that's hard to believe just wait a few seconds and notice that your thoughts are different from what they were a moment ago!

While tens of thousands of thoughts stream through your mind each day, the good news is it's been scientifically proven you can only have one thought at a time.[3]

Thoughts Are a Form of Currency

Having the capacity to only think one thought at a time is helpful, but the flip side is that each thought you have precludes having another one. Thoughts can be seen then as a form of currency where each one comes at a cost, because when you *pay* attention to one thing you spend time buying that experience and that time can never be replaced or recovered.

With this understanding comes the realization that your thoughts are a precious and limited resource.

HEAR THIS: Thoughts As Keyword

Your very own thoughts are the keywords and phrases that the Universe's Search Engine picks up, searches for, and returns matches to in the form of life experiences.

The Universe's Search Engine Delivers *Life Experiences*

Life experiences are occurrences in your everyday life that, in their totality, make up your quality of life. For instance, maybe you woke up this morning, went to the bathroom, brushed your teeth, washed your face, got dressed, made and ate breakfast, drove to work, worked, drove home, made and ate dinner, watched television, and did the dishes and a load of laundry before heading off to bed.

Obviously, this is an over-simplification of a day in the life. Color in what happens in between, like hearing from a childhood friend, getting a flat tire, someone buying you a coffee, getting test results, having a great lunch with your sister, or losing that promotion.

You Are Responsible

To demonstrate how the Universe's Search Engine returns matches in the form of real-life experiences, take the unfortunate story of a young woman who was kidnapped by a taxi driver and survived. When asked by reporters how she knew what to do she said it was simple, her mom had always told her what to do in case she was kidnapped by a taxi driver. Every time the mother told her daughter "how to escape from being kidnapped by a taxi driver," thoughts repeatedly broadcasted from both as they vividly imagined the scenario. Their thoughts are what precipitated the experience, and the Universe's Search Engine picked them up again and again, dutifully searching for a frequency match until finally it was delivered as a life experience.

Inspirational speaker and author Esther Hicks says it best in her book, *Ask and It Is Given.* "With enough attention to anything, the essence of what you have been giving thought to will eventually become a physical manifestation". Time and time again I've heard people say, "My worst fear is *<fill in the blank>*." Sadly, but not surprisingly given these scientific principles, I've seen their worst fear called to fruition. Maybe you've observed the same.

It may be difficult to grasp or accept that you are responsible for the life you're living today, but there is no doubt you are *constantly* emitting thoughts. The Universe's Search Engine is also a *constant*, continuously picking up your thoughts, searching for and returning vibratory frequency matches in the form of life experiences. It's pure science.

While the Universe's Search Engine delivers real-life experiences, it is not responsible for your quality of life. You are, because no one else can use your mind to think thoughts. You alone are the thinker of your mind, and it is your thoughts alone that trigger the search and the ensuing return of life experiences.

Feeling Bundles

The best tool at your disposal to clue you in to what you're thinking is your feelings. Feelings function as a global positioning system (GPS) or guidance system alerting you to what you're thinking about. As such, a direct indicator of your thoughts is your mood.

Besides clueing you into your thoughts, your feelings hitch a ride and *bundle* onto thoughts, intensifying emissions and transitioning weak searches or signals into strong ones. *Feeling Bundles*, as I've termed them, enable thoughts to travel faster on the frequency highway.

That matters because the intensity of your thoughts works like a boomerang: If you ever-so-gently toss one into the air without force it will fall to the ground because it lacks the velocity to work effectively. The strength of your throw determines the distance the boomerang travels, and speed in which it returns. The more intense the throw, the further it goes and the quicker it returns.

Like a boomerang, bundled thoughts have a more forceful trajectory and therefore travel faster on the frequency highway, returning matches sooner. The more intense your focus and feelings the quicker matches are returned in the form of life experiences.

However, while feeling bundles strengthen thought signals and increase velocity they do not change their vibratory frequency. For instance, the frequency of happy is still happy and the vibratory frequency of anger is still anger, regardless how intensely happy or extremely mad you are. Rather, attaching feeling bundles is like going from a decaf coffee to a double espresso, they're both coffee but one is more potent than the other.

Define What You Want

With the understanding that thoughts produced by firing neurons are responsible for bringing forth real-life experiences with feelings as super-chargers, your opportunity is to stop underutilizing and underestimating them and begin harnessing their power!

Where do you start? The first step is figuring out what's important to you, what makes you happy, and what you want out of life. Those answers inform where you should spend focused time broadcasting thoughts and attaching feeling bundles to increase trajectory and return matches sooner.

Expanded Thought Consciousness

After defining your desires the next step is to expand your thought consciousness, which means becoming more aware of what you're thinking and therefore entering as a search. Cultivating *self-awareness* assists in uncovering and better managing transmissions. And, as awareness grows, your competency in monitoring, recognizing, and pivoting thoughts increases. Given that success in becoming a deliberate creator is dependent on consciously managing your thoughts Chapter 6 is fully devoted to self-awareness tools and techniques.

You're Already a Master Creator

Since neurons are always firing, you've been producing and broadcasting thoughts throughout your entire lifetime. Those thoughts have been picked up and carried by the Universe's Search Engine in search of vibratory frequency matches rain or shine, day in and day out.

To see what the Universe's Search Engine has returned by way of real-life experiences (matching past thoughts), take a look around. What do you see? It's likely you have a comfortable home, maybe loving relationships, a car, a job, and so on.

So, don't let the prospect of becoming a deliberate creator frighten or intimidate you. You are already a well-seasoned master creator! The life you have today is directly correlated to all your bundled thoughts up to this point. You have been creating all along.

Your Superpower Is Your Birthright

Born as a transmitter with the capacity for your brain to emit thoughts with feeling bundles boosting their power, bundled thought transmission is your superpow*e*r!

Key Principles

1. You are pure energy.
2. Firing neurons create electromagnetic waves that emanate outwards as thoughts.
3. Thoughts are processed like keywords or phrases.
4. The Universe's Search Engine searches for vibrational matches to the keywords you've entered by way of thoughts.
5. The Universe's Search Engine returns real-life experiences based on what you have thought about.
6. You are responsible for your thoughts.
7. The vibratory frequencies of thoughts vary according to what you are thinking.
8. Your thoughts are finite, with each thought precluding another.
9. Feelings and your mood are indicators of what you're thinking about.
10. Feelings bundle onto thoughts, increasing trajectory and bringing forth matches sooner.
11. Determine what you want and spend time broadcasting that to the Universe.
12. Use self-awareness to observe and manage your thoughts.
13. You're already a master creator.
14. Bundled thought transmission is your superpower.

CHAPTER 3
QUANTUM PHYSICS MATTERS

*"Science, through Quantum Physics, is showing us
that everything in our Universe is energy."*
– Comillo Lokin

Learning how thoughts, feelings, and the Universe's Search Engine work together to deliver your quality of life is incredibly helpful. The same insight applies when you gain an understanding of a few basic laws of physics because they similarly impact your life in a huge way.

You Already Know QP

While the words "quantum physics" might send you running for the hills, stick with me and you'll be surprised how much you already know! For instance, the *law of vibration* states: If you were to break down anything to its purest form and analyze it—seen or unseen—you would find pure energy resonating as a *vibratory frequency*. In Chapter 1: Pillars 1 and 2, we covered how matter is pure energy in a constant state of motion in the form of vibrational frequencies.

Another quantum physics principle states: Thoughts are things that hold the energy field into what it is you see. In Chapter 2 we covered how the Universe's Search Engine a) picks up thoughts as keywords and b) searches for, then c) returns frequency matches in the form of real-life experiences. This is how your thoughts bring to you what you see.

The Law of Attraction

I'd guess the most popular law of physics is the Law of Attraction, which is the magnetic power of the Universe that draws similar energies together. The 2006 Australian-American documentary, *The Secret*, taught us that life experiences are formed through our thoughts and related emotions. Exactly what we're talking about!

That film did a great job of kicking off the discussion on our journey to expanded consciousness and harnessing universal powers. This book picks up where it left off, putting the pieces together to decipher precisely how, in scientific terms, the Law of Attraction works.

HEAR THIS: Law of Attraction Is the Frequency Highway

If you've read Chapters 1 and 2 you already know how the Law of Attraction works, because I theorize that: The Law of Attraction *and* the frequency highway are one and the same.

- LAW OF ATTRACTION: THE MAGNETIC POWER OF THE UNIVERSE THAT DRAWS SIMILAR ENERGIES TOGETHER
- FREQUENCY HIGHWAY: THE CONDUIT THAT BRINGS TOGETHER MATCHING FREQUENCIES

The force behind both the frequency highway and Law of Attraction is the same, functioning to bring together "similar energies" or "matching frequencies." The secret has been hiding in plain sight all along, camouflaged in semantics. Science cracks the code, making what was once ambiguous tangible, accessible, and harnessable!

Understanding that the frequency highway and Law of Attraction both function as the Universe's Search Engine, and deliberately harnessing that knowledge to better manage your thoughts to control what's returned is enough to dramatically improve your quality of life.

But there's much more to share about harnessing its power to return your dream life, so we continue.

Entrainment

Universally speaking, frequencies work to harmonize. This relates to another quantum physics principle, *entrainment*, which states: The natural state of being is in harmony.

You notice entrainment when someone yawns and it makes you yawn, or when someone claps or laughs how others join in even if they don't know what they're clapping or laughing for. The same thing happens when someone smiles at you and you smile back no matter how bad your day is going. Entrainment takes the credit for these automatic responses.

Entrainment works on a molecular level within our bodies as well. The synching of menstrual cycles when women spend a fair amount of time with each other is an incredible yet quite a common phenomenon.

Entrainment applies to inanimate objects too. The most dramatic example comes from a scientific study conducted by Dutch physicist Christiaan Huygens in 1665 that positioned two grandfather clocks side-by-side with their pendulums swinging at different rates. Entrainment caused the pendulums to become synchronized within one day.

Law of Least Resistance

Continuing with the theme of harmony, the *law of least resistance* is related to nature where electrons always choose the path of least resistance. You can apply this law to your life by letting go of opposition and opting for self-resolution, refraining from taking any action and allowing a situation to resolve on its own.

Some evoke conscious passiveness as a way to apply this principle. While the word "passive" tends to have a negative connotation, here *choosing* to be passive is a Jedi mind trick where you no longer resist and instead consciously move into trusting that a situation will work out in its own time and manner, accepting the outcome whatever it may be. In this way it's possible to do nothing and accomplish more, which is why this law is also known as the *law of least effort*.

In my job managing a portfolio of high-tech *Fortune* 500 companies I had an opportunity to leverage conscious passiveness. A choppy implementation led to a horde of daily fire drills with high priority issues needing my immediate attention. Dutifully, I rolled up my sleeves and dug in, giving it all I had. But when the intense pressure and breakneck pace didn't let up after several months I became completely overwhelmed. In tears, I strongly considered submitting my resignation. However, the timing coincided with a planned vacation, so I made the decision to reevaluate upon my return.

During my trip I let it all go, enjoying time with my family and meditating daily. When I returned to work a week later, I had renewed energy and clarity. This afforded me the ability to lean into conscious passiveness. What did that look like? As the avalanche of emails poured in, rather than *reactively* responding, I first checked with my gut to see if I had an interest in engaging. For roughly 80% of the onslaught, I found I didn't. So I selected conscious passiveness and said, "Nope, I'm not going to touch that." Then I deleted those emails.

If that sounds crazy, I completely understand because doing less and accomplishing more is the polar opposite of what many of us were taught. It's counter intuitive, and yet, like gravity, the law of least resistance is a universal law that always holds true. With faith in all universal principles I decided to eat my own dog food (switching the polarity, drink my own Champaign). I took an educated leap of faith, trusting in the power of the law of least resistance and utilized conscious passiveness.

On the heels of deleting numerous emails I immediately asked myself, "What would make me happy? What do I want to do?" Then I'd do it! Often, it was as simple as going outside to walk the property and take in the magnificence of the flowers and majestic trees. Sometimes I preferred to meditate, and other times I felt like loving on my dogs. These activities brought me peace, balance, and wellbeing, so I continued with this approach for the entire week, day after day checking in with my gut for what would make me happy and choosing conscious passiveness and self-resolution.

By week's end I noticed a desire. I felt inspired to re-engage, so I delved into my inbox. Wouldn't you know it? The vast majority—nearly 80%—of what came in throughout the week had self-resolved (mostly by way of different directions taken). Indeed, it is possible to do nothing and accomplish more. What a joy!

As a caveat, for those whose work requires hands-on action (like a chef, ambulance driver, or doctor), your opportunity may not be to decide not to cook, drive, or mend someone. Instead, do a gut check to become aware of your feelings (as an indicator of your thoughts), and where friction or negative feelings exist make shifts by using the power of your thoughts to bring the joy. Stay tuned for Chapters 10 and 11, which offer practical guidance on living in joy when it appears your situation isn't allowing you to do so.

Ride the Current of Least Resistance

Fighting against what is elongates suffering, makes an issue bigger, and squanders your valuable energy.

During our honeymoon in Maui, my husband, John, and I took boogie boards out into the ocean. Unbeknownst to us, we had entered the water where there was a strong undercurrent that quickly pulled us towards the deep sea. Neither of us are seasoned swimmers so when I turned and noticed how far away we were from the shoreline I panicked and started yelling, "Turn around!" We both began kicking fiercely towards land but our best efforts netted no forward movement, and we continued being pulled away.

John recalled seeing a *20/20* episode that told the story of a college football player swept away by a riptide. Sadly, despite his youth and strength, after exerting all of his energy fighting against the current he drowned. The show intended to teach people caught in undercurrents to always swim parallel to the shore to move outside of the current, as fighting against it would prove futile.

At more than four hundred feet out John yelled to paddle parallel to the shore. As we did, soon resistance ceased. Not only were we no longer being pulled away, we'd entered into another current that effortlessly propelled us towards the beach.

This mimics what happens when you fight against what is. You expend more energy and get nowhere—maybe even further behind! Instead, leverage the quantum physics law of least resistance to move out of opposition and change the current.

Change the Channel

I offer a final example to further highlight how to move into harmony with the law of least effort when it looks like things aren't going your way. One Friday, my sixteen-year-old daughter, Skye, needed a ride home from her summer internship in the heart of Silicon Valley. While the commute in the Bay Area is always congested, Fridays are particularly brutal. I had thought about scheduling an Uber because traffic is my kryptonite. I am a cool-headed, loving, and kind individual until I'm behind the wheel where I turn into a laser-focused pilot on a mission to get wherever I'm going as efficiently, decisively, and quickly as possible. When my husband told me he'd pick her up I dismissed my anxieties. Then at the very last minute he wasn't able to go, so the chore returned to me.

To relieve some of the burden, we agreed to meet up at a restaurant located between her job and our home. I arrived at the agreed upon location right on time and texted Skye to see how close she was.

When she replied that she hadn't left the office yet, and it would be more than an hour before she did, it's fair to say I was frustrated and disappointed. As a self-proclaimed energy snob, I saw this delay as a waste of my precious time.

Although I knew I was exuding negative bundled thoughts, I nevertheless remained pretty steamy. Recognizing a need to make a shift, I went over my options and decided to pick Skye up so I could be in control of the situation. As my attention returned to the navigation screen I saw solid red depicting standstill traffic in every direction. Knowing negative vibes were beaming out of me, I asked myself, "What can I do to change this? *What would make me happy?*"

I decided to listen to Alanis Morissette because singing my heart out to her songs always makes me feel really good. As I nudged back onto the freeway inch-by-inch, singing "Uninvited," sure enough my vibratory frequency lifted and I began feeling happy. By the time I reached Skye, forty-five minutes later, I was shoulder dancing and smiling, emitting high vibes full blast.

Find Your Happy

When Skye jumped into the car she was unhappy with my music choice and immediately began complaining. I explained that I needed to do something to cheer myself up, and added, "Find your way to be happy." She picked the next song and proceeded to belt it out. We ended up having so much fun in stop-and-go traffic! Along with good practice in energy conversion and an unexpectedly good time, we both came out of that long, slow car ride with memories that'll last forever.

The takeaway is, in all cases you have the power of choice to decide if you want to be upset and view a situation as a nightmare, or look for and find the hidden gift(s). You get to elect how you receive the energy that's coming at you, and choose what you do with it.

Your Jedi Moves

Pay attention to your feelings because they're your key indicator alerting you to what you're thinking about, and therefore exuding. Take responsibility for the role you play as the creator of your life experiences and when you find yourself angry or having other negative feelings or thoughts, acknowledge and thank them before asking, "What can I do to change this?"

Think constructively and harness the law of least resistance to move your energy into something positive and meaningful.

Invisible Matters

When it comes down to it, the secrets of the Universe aren't secrets at all; they're just invisible to the human eye. There are countless books and videos on this very subject matter. Each author does their best to explain these universal principles, motivated by a sincere desire to help others wield their powers to live a better, more joyous life. Yet for centuries these scientific principles have failed to move into the mainstream. Why is this? I believe it's primarily the *intangibility* that challenges comprehension and adoption.

If the invisibility of the Universe's Search Engine, bundled thoughts, and quantum physics principles makes it difficult for you to embrace, consider that even the tangible goes unseen sometimes. For instance, stars are invisible during the day, but they certainly exist at all times. You can't see gravity or love, but we are sure of their existence and to ignore them would be detrimental to your life experience.

The same applies here. Don't let the invisibility of proven universal laws be an impediment to leveraging these powerful, life-changing principles to their fullest to create the life of your most fantastical dreams!

Key Principles

1. The Law of Attraction and the frequency highway are one and the same.
2. The Universe's Search Engine returns life experiences that match the frequency of thoughts (aka keywords).
3. Everything in the Universe emits vibrational frequencies, including thoughts.
4. Frequencies work to harmonize, known as entrainment.
5. The law of least resistance relates to electrons choosing the path of least resistance.
6. Pivot negative frequencies to positive through awareness, then asking what you can do to change the situation.
7. Pay attention to feelings as your guidance system indicating the frequencies you're emitting.
8. The invisible forces of nature matter.

CHAPTER 4
MANIFESTATION MATTERS

*"Since the universe and everything in it is energy,
mind power works on the principle that if you match
your frequency to what it is you desire, it has no
choice but to become, since like attracts like."*
–Stephen Richards

With a firm understanding of the universal laws that bring forth life experiences across science, energy, and quantum physics, we can now turn our attention to leveraging these principles to improve any or all aspects of your life.

The Universe's Search Engine is perfectly perfect at its job, never failing to pick up, search for, and return real-life experiences that match what you've searched for by way of your thoughts. So what's happening when your desires aren't being fulfilled? What's up with that?

Manifestation Requires a Vibrational Match

Since the Universe's Search Engine brings matching frequencies together, you may have already guessed that the key ingredient in manifesting is matching the frequency of your thoughts to the frequency of your desires. And you'd be right!

Imagine you became more specific about what you wanted,

deciding you would love to buy a new home. That's a great thought to exude! Along with your excitement, however, you are *afraid* that you might *lose your job* and *wouldn't be able to pay* the mortgage, which could snowball into *losing everything.* You also *worry* about being *house poor.* You've had friends that were and always imagined it to be *a horrible way to live.*

In this example, can you see how you are out of range of being a vibrational match to your desire? Your thoughts about fear, worry, loss and lack completely override your excitement, impacting the frequency of your initially positive thought.

Let's dissect this bundled thought and get granular on what's going on here:

- **Keywords and Phrases:**
  o **Thought:** I want to buy a new house + visualize a horrible way to live = Frequency mismatch
  o **Feeling bundles:**
    a. ↑ Positive bundle: Excitement for a new home
    b. ↓ Negative bundles: Fear and worry about loss and lack
       i. Loss:
          1. ↓ Losing your job
          2. ↓ Losing everything
       ii. Lack:
          1. ↓ Not enough money to pay the mortgage
          2. ↓ Being house poor

- **Universe's Search Engine:**
  o **Searches for a match:** Desire to own a home + visualizing a horrible way to live + bundles of excitement, loss^2, lack^2
  o **Returns a match:** Find a home but lose your job so not enough money to purchase it

In contrast, a vibrational match for the desire of owning a home looks like this:

I've decided to buy a new house and I'm so excited about it! I'm very fortunate that I have a job so *I can definitely afford it*. I am a bit worried about the unknowns, but others have done it so *I'm sure I can too*. I know *things always work out for me*. I can't wait to have our first Christmas in our new home. I can already see Joey's and Cindy's stockings hanging on the fireplace!

- **Keywords and Phrases:**
  - o **Thought:** I want to buy a new house + visualize Christmas in your new home = Frequency match
  - o **Feeling bundles:**
    - a) ↑ Positive bundles:
      1. ↑ Excitement for a new home
      2. ↑ Appreciation for job
    - b) Uncertainty bundle: A bit of worry but when sensed shifted to trust, so negative *scratched* by shift to positive

Now the Universe's Search Engine steps up to do its job. Here's what that looks like:

- **Universe's Search Engine:**
  - o **Searches for a match**: Desire to own a home + visualizing Christmas in your new home + bundles of excitement, appreciation, and joyful experiences
  - o **Returns match** (provided no underlying mismatching frequencies): Purchase the home, keep your job, hang stockings on the mantel

Can you feel the difference in vibrational energy as you read through those two examples? In either scenario it's important to recognize that the Universe's Search Engine did exactly what you commanded of it, returning a match to what you've "searched for."

Let's play around with a couple more examples related to abundance, or lack thereof. Say you're thinking about wealth in the form of how wonderful it is that you have enough money to pay your bills. The Universe's Search Engine a) picks up those thoughts,

b) searches for frequency matches to *wealth*, and c) returns a life experience in the form of a raise.

Take the opposite polarity and say you're thinking about lack in the form of never having enough money to pay your bills. The Universe's Search Engine a) picks up, b) searches for frequency matches to *lack*, and c) returns a life experience in the form of your rent increasing.

Again, in either scenario the Universe's Search Engine returned matches to what you "searched for."

Focus on What You Want, Not the Absence of It

Of course, no one intentionally "searches" for an increase in rent, but often when you think you're focusing on what you want you're really thinking about the absence of it. For instance, "I *don't want* to be broke" is the frequency of lack and focuses on what you *don't want*. That low frequency is why you don't feel good when you focus here.

On the other hand, "I *do want* to be wealthy" is the frequency of wealth and focuses on what you *do want*. Wealth is a high frequency, which is why you feel good when you focus here.

While they may seem the same, the frequency of what you want versus what you do not want are opposite in polarity and therefore summon very different experiences. What you focus on expands, so think about what's wanted, and not the lack aspect of it.

Sync Needed

I offer a final illustration using integrating two technologies to describe frequency matching. When you want to pair your cell phone with a car's audio system you go into "Settings" in your phone and turn on "Bluetooth." Your phone then sends a signal over the frequency highway (aka the Universe's Search Engine) and there is an attempt to pair with your car's audio system. If the frequencies match a connection is established, but if there's no match the process is blocked and no sync occurs.

In order for an experience to occur there must be a sync between the vibrational frequency of your thoughts *and* the frequency of the life experiences you are seeking. There must be a match on both sides.

The Trap Door

Because the Universe's Search Engine does its job unquestioningly the matches to your desires have already been found and are available to you. If they haven't shown up yet they are simply waiting for you to finish pairing.

Imagine all of the desires you've ever had in a holding room with a trap door in the floor, and get this … the trap door is held shut with a very old and worn piece of tape that's barely hanging on. It cannot wait to break free, which it will do as soon as you become a vibrational match to the frequency of your desire. When the vibratory match is achieved, the trap door bursts open and your desires are manifested. As fairytale-like as this may sound, it's scientific law and can be no other way. I've seen it occur time and time again where manifestation goes from nowhere to now-here.

PART A: INTENSIFIERS

In Chapter 2 you learned how feeling bundles attach to thoughts and intensify their emissions. This section shares additional intensifiers to help expedite the return of your desires.

Desires

If a desire has been inspired within you then there's an absolute ability of that desire to come to fruition.[4] By virtue of simply having that desire you have expanded yourself from who you were to the potentiality of who you can be. For instance, I see myself as a sought-after keynote speaker evolving how people think, resulting in dramatically improving the quality of life of audiences globally. This desire was a thought that activated and expanded my capacity for more while emanating new vibrational frequencies that the Universe's Search Engine picked up and began seeking matches to return.

Desires are thoughts accompanied by feelings like hope and excitement. As intensifiers, those feelings bundle onto thoughts resulting in greater trajectory onto the frequency highway. This velocity works to prioritize your thoughts with a higher ranking, therefore expediting manifestation.

If you have trouble determining what your best life looks like, reflect on the things that make you happy. Ask, "What would I wish for if I had three wishes, or all the money in the world and unlimited time?" If that doesn't work think about someone else's life that you wish you had, narrowing in on what it is about their life that you would want. What do you admire about it? What makes their life so great? What is it that they have that you don't? Finally, try recalling in your mind's eye who you hoped you'd grow up to be.

Dream. Dream Bigger. Is That All You Got?

Once you know what you wish for, pump it up! Take your desires and make them grander by aiming higher. Here's what that looks like:

- **My dream**: Take a weeklong vacation to Bora Bora.
- **Dream bigger**: Take a two-week vacation to Bora Bora, flying first class.
- **Is that all you got?**: Take a month-long vacation to the Fijian islands with my extended family, rent a chartered yacht for a week with full staff, and have a private concert from Alanis Morrisette.

Reaching for the moon alters your trajectory so you end up reaching higher heights. Go ahead and push your ideas to crazy-way-out-there and have fun with it! With its extraordinarily high vibration, having *fun* is like coating your thoughts with a *slick emollient*, enabling them to effortlessly glide on the frequency highway to bring forth speedier results (figure 11).

Figure 11: Fun coats thoughts with a slick emollient, expediting fruition.

A Thought, First

Everything that is was a thought first. For instance, pick any chair in your home. Before the chair became yours it was in a store, and before that it was at a manufacturer, and prior to that it was some kind of drawing or plan, and before that it was in someone's head, as a thought.

Since everything that is must be a thought first, it's important to get clear about what your best life looks like.

COMPLETE EXERCISE 1: DEFINE WHAT YOU WANT

- Description: Clarify and prioritize your desires.
- Time allocation: 30 minutes
- Page 149
- Online: anitamscott.com/ex1— Password (case sensitive): desire

---

Investment Needed

Once you have that clarity, investment is needed by way of spending time on focused thinking, imagining, obtaining, and living in your perfect future state.

In addition to focused thinking sometimes inspired action is needed. For instance, if you want to become a doctor the Universe's Search Engine has lanes to that desired outcome, but if you don't invest resources by way of time, energy, or money likely you will not become a doctor and that trap door will never open. The "Meet Me Halfway" parable characterizes this well:

Paul, who was in financial difficulty, walked into a church and started to pray. "Listen God,'" Paul said. "I know I haven't been perfect but I really need to win the lottery. I don't have a lot of money. Please help me out." He left the church, a week went by, and he hadn't won the lottery, so he walked into a synagogue. "Come on, God," he said. "I really need this money. My mom needs surgery and I have bills to pay. Please let me win the lottery."

He left the synagogue, a week went by, and he didn't win the lottery. So, he went to a mosque and started to pray again. "You're starting to disappoint me, God," he said. "I've prayed and prayed. If you just let me win the lottery, I'll be a better person. I don't have to win the jackpot, just enough to get me out of debt. I'll give some to charity, even. Just let me win the lottery." Paul thought this did it, so he got up and walked outside.

The clouds opened up and a booming voice said, "Paul, buy a freaking lottery ticket."[5]

Do yourself a favor and take inspired action to achieve your desires. Taking *inspired action* is like coating your bundled thoughts with *rocket fuel*, propelling you forward on your chosen lane (figure 12).

Figure 12: Inspired actions coat thoughts with rocket fuel increasing velocity.

Visualization Fires Motor Neurons

Using your imagination to visualize is another powerful tool in expediting the return of your desires. Here's the science behind why that is: When you take any physical action motor neurons fire up at the front of your brain. Besides emitting electromagnetic waves, firing motor neurons also trigger nerve impulses responsible for producing your body's movement. What's cool is when you visualize, these same motor neurons fire even when you don't move a muscle.

In 1984, Russian scientists proved this phenomenon by assessing four groups of Olympic athletes using different combinations of physical and visualization training:

- Group 1: Practiced 0% visualization, 100% physical training
- Group 2: Practiced 25% visualization, 75% physical training
- Group 3: Practiced 50% visualization, 50% physical training
- Group 4: Practiced 75% visualization, 25% physical training

Remarkably the last group performing only 25% physical training did the best, achieving better results than those putting in three times the amount of physical practice.[6]

How can this be? The Olympian's visualizations fired motor neurons *as if they were* physically running the races. In so doing these athletes had the opportunity to experience running their races in ideal form time and time again, imagining every detail of the perfect technique over and over. They also had the benefit of repeatedly picturing themselves—visualizing themselves—crossing the finish line first.

When you visualize you produce frequencies that are in the same vibratory frequency of your desired state. It's like *visualization* encases thoughts in *magic sparkle dust* (figure 13).

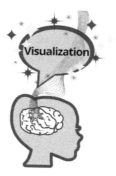

Figure 13: Visualizing your future state encases thoughts in magic sparkle dust, producing frequencies that match the frequency of your desires.

Priming the Universe's Search Engine

Besides growing confidence, these Olympic athletes practiced visualization repeatedly produced and broadcasted thoughts that primed the Universe's Search Engine, so during the actual race their vibrational frequency synched with their practiced desire, and the tape broke free on that trap door. When you understand the laws of science and physics it isn't so surprising. They simply combined the power of their thoughts with the power of visualization.

If you're worried you can't or don't know how to visualize, when you're remembering a past experience and see pictures in your head, or when you imagine something by forming mental images you are visualizing.

Live in Your Future-State Now

When you imagine living in the space of already accomplishing your dream life, you emit powerful bundled thoughts that match (or are at least in the vibratory vicinity of) your desires.

I'll model how I go about doing this. I close my eyes and think about how this book was published by a world-renowned publisher. I'm filled with appreciation that *The Universe is Your Search Engine* resonated with so many readers. I see myself presenting keynotes on every continent and I'm filled with delight that the information has vastly improved the quality of life of audiences and readers alike, ultimately raising the vibratory frequency of the planet. I move into the space of pure joy. I'm so happy I can't contain myself so I stand up and dance around. My excitement overflows!

Stand up and dance around? Oh yes I did! Neurons fired, feelings exuded, my body moved and away those bundled thoughts zoomed.

Now you try. What do you wish would happen for you? Close your eyes and imagine it's happening right now. Immerse yourself in rich details as if you have actualized your desired state. Is your heart so big it feels like it will burst? What do you see? What does it feel like in your stomach? Exactly how big is the smile on your face? That! That's what it feels like to be a frequency match to your desire. In this space the Universe will conspire to bring it to you. This is law. Trap door open!

Give It a Voice

Have you ever experienced mulling over a problem for some time and then one day when you said it out loud, *hearing* yourself say the words gave you clarity and made all the difference in the world? Thinking something is one thing, but saying it is another.

Remember, your voice emits sound waves that are vibrational frequencies. When you add your voice to thoughts *sound wave bundles* attach, acting like multipliers, increasing its intensity and therefore momentum (figure 14).

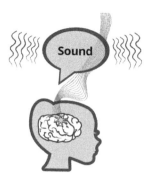

Figure 14: Sound wave intensifiers bundle onto thoughts, increasing momentum.

The Power of Intention

Another tremendously powerful tool at your disposal to better control and expedite what the Universe's Search Engine returns is setting intentions. Intention setting is a force of nature, so when you intend something it's far more likely to come to bear.

Researcher and photographer Dr. Masaru Emoto exposed water to different pictures, music and words (written and spoken), then froze the water and took microscopic pictures. The results were nothing short of amazing! Upon examination, the images showed positive terms like "thank you," "angel," "truth," "spirit," "love," and "gratitude" rendered beautiful crystal shapes. Conversely, negative terms like "evil," "you fool," and "you disgust me" rendered the crystals ugly, discolored, and frightening.[7]

In a later unrelated study, a group in Australia was instructed to send intentions to a control group of seeds in the United States to "be healthy and grow faster." Indeed, the targeted group of seeds grew higher and faster than the seeds where no intentions were placed. Another study performed years later yielded the same results when a control group was directed to send their intentions *online*![8]

Your Thoughts Impact Others

Since Dr. Emoto's research was published more than two decades ago there have been many more intention experiments, all resulting in the same conclusion. Besides creating your life experiences, your thoughts also have the power to impact things outside of you.

So how is it that someone can send an intention to something—in this case seeds—from the other side of the world or through a computer and the intended recipient is affected? How exactly does that work?

HEAR THIS: Intentions Act as Shipping Labels

When someone focuses and directs an intention to one thing, their transmitted thoughts are picked up by the Universe's Search Engine. This we already know. What's next is new: When you use the power of intention with a targeted recipient in mind, it's like placing a shipping label directly onto your thought. That shipping label informs the Universe's Search Engine exactly where to deliver your exuded vibrations.

Can you see how attaching a recipient's address would speed things up? With 1) an intention defined (be healthy and grow faster), and 2) a receiver determined (seeds in the U.S.), those thoughts are rendered lean, aerodynamic, and free from ambiguity, thus enabling them to sail across the frequency highway expeditiously to deliver specific vibratory frequencies to the intended target.

HEAR THIS: Vibratory Frequency Decoders and Absorbers

The intended recipient receives the transmitted thoughts and decodes it back into your intended wish. In the case of the seed experiment, to be healthy and grow faster. The recipient literally absorbs your vibrational frequencies, which impacts its vibratory frequency. This is how the seeds did, in fact, grow healthier and faster.

Anything that produces a vibratory frequency has the functionality installed to *decode and absorb thoughts*. This means, your thoughts can also be sent, received, and absorbed by other people. As a transmitter and receiver, you emit and receive vibes simultaneously.

Let's take a mini-pause here because there are a number of significant concepts happening back-to-back:

1. Everything in the Universe has a vibrational frequency receiver and decoder (including water, seeds, and you).
2. Thoughts are literal emissions that can be sent, received, and absorbed.
3. The vibrational frequency of thoughts impacts the receiver's vibratory frequency.

Besides having the power to draw forth life experiences, there is undisputed scientific proof that thoughts also have the capacity to influence other's vibratory frequencies.

CONNECTING THE DOTS: Emissions from Matter Impacts You

Let's take a moment to connect some dots here. In the first chapter we learned that all matter exudes information. Given that everything in the Universe is equipped with receivers and decoders, it follows that *information has the ability to impact our vibrations too.*

To understand how, think about a time when you were in nature and how good it felt. That's not a coincidence. Since information emanates continuously from all matter, when you're in nature you are impacted by emissions from trees, bushes, grass, and flowers all of which are broadcasting wellness, vitality, and the joy of being. Absorbing their emissions, which are bursting with positive, healing vibes, is what makes you feel so good and why some say nature has healing powers.

It's also why research has proven that having even just one plant in a room has a significant impact on reducing stress and anxiety.[9] It's thanks to our ability to absorb matter's emissions.

Vibratory Frequency of Intentions

There's another gold nugget to mine about intention setting. Take a moment to think about what setting an intention *feels* like. What do you intend to do when you put this book down. Maybe take a nap or a shower? When you go to work tomorrow what do you intend to accomplish? If you work in business likely you intend to get through all of your emails, finish building a presentation, and hold a few meetings.

Notice intentions have a very different flavor and vary greatly from the frequency of an idea. An intention is a goal, plan, or decision that turns thoughts into actions (rocket fuel).

Intentions bundle onto thoughts like an arrowhead with a razor sharp tip coated with a special sauce that's irresistible to the Universe to conspire and bring it to you (figure 15).

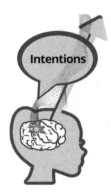

Figure 15: Intentions bundle onto thoughts like a razor sharp arrowhead facilitating increased trajectory.

Setting Intentions

The first step in leveraging the power of intention is to determine what your intentions are. From there simply state, "I intend to *<add in your intended outcome>*." Then visualize the outcome and nurture it in your heart, reveling in the feelings.

Not surprisingly, a habit of highly successful people is the practice of seeing themselves one to five years in the future, setting intentions often to evolve into what they imagine their best life looks like. Their success is no accident! They harness a trifecta of mental powers:

THOUGHTS + VISUALIZATION + INTENTION SETTING

When you set intentions the Universe devises to orchestrate and deliver all of the cooperative components to help you achieve what you've set out to accomplish. The Universe always meets you at the intersection of your commitment and intention.

Power in the People

Group intention setting is another powerful multiplier. When 1) numerous thoughts with the same vibratory frequency are exuded 2) at the same time 3) to the same intended target, momentum and signal strength increases.

Prayer groups have been known to achieve miraculous results since the recipient absorbs numerous powerful healing vibes. When you understand how thoughts, the Universe's Search Engine, quantum physics and intentions work you know that, while wondrous indeed, those miracles are facilitated by the principles of science and physics.

Having others hold an intention for you is also a multiplier, making your desire likelier to come to fruition based on the same premise. When others hold your intention they carry your desire in their hearts and visualize you in the achievement of your desired state. To leverage this power, share your intention(s) and give permission for others to hold them for you.

Word Matters

When we discussed Dr. Emoto's water experiment we focused on intentions, but there's one final treasure here. When you see the images you notice different words impacted the water in different ways, with each word producing unique crystal structures. This quite literally shows us that every word also has its own distinct frequency.

With the power to affect the structure of water *outside* of your body, imagine the impact words have on your own cells, which are comprised primarily of water! What you say resonates throughout every cell of your body.

PART B: MINIMIZERS

Negative and positive are different sides of the same coin, so if there are intensifiers and multipliers like emollient (fun), rocket fuel (action), sparkle dust (visualization), sound waves (voice) and arrowheads (intentions) that bundle onto thoughts, then there are minimizers too. This section reveals a few so you can steer clear.

Mismatch Creates Static

You know (now) that the life you have today is directly correlated to the thoughts you've had in the past. Accepting your current life situation is of utmost importance because non-acceptance demonstrates resistance, and according to the quantum physics law of least resistance what you resist persists.

Non-acceptance, or frustration over what is, also introduces *static*. Static produced from the "dissatisfaction with now" interferes with becoming a vibrational match to your future desired state, effectively slowing down manifestation. In fact, discontentment with "what is" could block manifestation altogether.

To achieve harmony and balance make peace with what's bothering you by moving into acceptance. Look for and find the *perfection of now*. Utilize appreciation for what is going well, and focus only on the positive aspects of your life to get further faster.

COMPLETE EXERCISE 2: RAISE YOUR FREQUENCY

- Description: Use the power of gratitude to reduce static and increase your frequency.
- Time allocation: 20 minutes
- Page 151
- Online: anitamscott.com/ex2 – Password (case sensitive): raise

---

Gestation Period

Often you'll experience a period of lag time between a wish or thought, and the manifestation of it. During this lull time you're unable to see that progress is being made by way of you becoming more and cooperative components being gathered. Esther Hicks says new desires are like planting a seed of corn, where gestation time is necessary for the corn to sprout, grow, and produce ears of corn. You don't expect to plant the seed and then continuously say, "Where is my corn?"

If you spend time worrying and wondering why 'it's' not here yet, you introduce static, exuding vibes of lack that can continuously hold you at arms distance from achievement of your desired state. Do your best to focus on what you want and not the absence of it so your vibrational frequency is in harmony with your desires.

Ambiguity

Decades ago I used to say, "I just want to be happy." Eventually, I realized so does everyone else. Have you ever known someone to say otherwise? Using "I just want to be happy" is lazy. Don't get me wrong, being content and not wanting for much is a fine way of being. John Lennon said of being happy, "When I was five years old, my mother always told me that happiness was the key to life. When I went to school, they asked me what I wanted to be when I grew up. I wrote down 'happy.' They told me I didn't understand the assignment, and I told them they didn't understand life."

On the other hand, the state of "being of happy" is a goal. It's what you aspire to be. The question then is: *What makes you happy?* If you have a sketchy idea but aren't really sure about what you want, your signals are too weak to return a match. In the same way that entering the keyword "next" into Google nets you more than five million results, "I just want to be happy" is much too vague. It works like a magic paint, effectively rendering the thought invisible to the Universe's Search Engine.

Simply put, you're not emitting thoughts about your dream life if you don't know what that looks like. Get clear and be decisive about what fills you with joy. That clarity of desire removes ambiguity, which is why it's the first step to becoming a deliberate creator. Only you can know what your best life looks like.

Self-Limiting

Once you hone in on what you desire and what you intend to manifest, leave some room. Being too prescriptive can blind you from seeing other opportunities in the same vibrational vicinity.

For instance, say you narrow in on a wish to move into a new apartment in a particular neighborhood and you begin visualizing a two-bedroom, two-bathroom apartment with an orange door. When a two bedroom, two bathroom detached home with an orange door becomes available in the right neighborhood and within your price range, you completely ignore it because of the specificity of an "apartment."

Often what's returned can be better than what you envision for yourself, so leave plenty of room for the divergence.

Limiting Belief Systems

If you are living life just getting by on paltry scraps it's almost certain that belief systems are responsible. Belief systems are one of the biggest impediments to living a full, productive, happy, and healthy life. So let's talk about them.

In their infancy belief systems were *prescribed thoughts* that our parents, clergy, teachers or other authority figures used to teach us right from wrong, according to what they were taught. As children we lack the cognitive ability to question, so those teachings became hardwired programs that heavily influence how we live our lives and operate in the world as adults.

See if any of the following belief systems sound familiar:

- MONEY DOESN'T GROW ON TREES
- YOU CAN'T HAVE EVERYTHING YOU WANT
- THE WORLD IS A CRUEL PLACE
- THE EARLY BIRD GETS THE WORM
- EDUCATION IS THE KEY TO SUCCESS
- IN ORDER TO SUCCEED YOU HAVE TO WORK HARD
- IF YOU DON'T PUSH HARD NOTHING WILL HAPPEN
- GIRLS ARE FEMININE
- BOYS ARE MASCULINE
- YOU MUST BE SAVED
- YOU MUST BE X RELIGION TO BE SAVED
- THERE IS A HEAVEN AND HELL

These and other deeply engrained patterns of thought can keep you stuck by giving the illusion that you can't change your mind.

While thoughts are fluid, belief systems are thoughts that have turned into a solid, forming a blockage that prevents you from seeing life as it truly is. Many belief systems, marriage for instance, are societal norms, but some can be like malignant masses spreading across every facet of your life, keeping you minimized and poisoning your ability to live your best life. I speak from experience. When I was seven my family adopted a new religion that brought with it a belief that the world was going to end, first in 1975, then in 1978, and thereafter destruction was imminent. I was taught that all the wicked people would be destroyed, and while I didn't believe I was wicked, I didn't know that I was "good enough" or "better than" so my expectation was I would die when Armageddon came.

Fast-forward two decades and I'm a divorced single-mom with no college education, working a dead-end job. Every night I come home and lie on my couch exhausted from a full day's work while my son, Grayson, plays outside. One night, while thinking about how I want more for us it finally occurs to me that I'm still alive! I start asking myself "what if" questions like, *"What if* the world isn't going to end? *What if* I get to live for another year, or two? *What if* my life is a gift?"

Soon after, I enrolled in college. Since then, I have earned three degrees, been happily married for more than twenty years, and have a beautiful family. My first book, *Greater Than Grateful,* recounts the full story, but in short, asking those "what if" questions melted away the paralyzing programming of my youth and gave me the capacity to start harnessing the power of my thoughts to control what the Universe's Search Engine returned. My quality of life has dramatically improved across every facet.

If you were to perform a diagnostic on why your thoughts aren't matching up with the frequencies of your desires, at the core most likely you'd find belief systems. The good news is you too can dissolve stifling programs by first uncovering them, and then asking "what if" questions like I did to melt them away.

COMPLETE EXERCISE 3: CHALLENGE YOUR BELIEF SYSTEMS

- Description: Identify and dissolve beliefs holding you back.
- Time allocation: 25 minutes
- Page 153
- Online: <u>anitamscott.com/ex3</u> – Password (case sensitive): dissolve

Self-Fulfilling Prophecy

A self-fulfilling prophecy is a prediction made by *you* that *you* inadvertently cause to come true. Belief systems are at the heart of all self-fulfilling prophecies because there's an expectation that what you believe is the truth, even when it is nothing more than a belief.

An example of a self-fulfilling prophecy is when someone believes in Murphy's Law, which states: Anything that can go wrong will go wrong. That belief is a thought that predisposes an expectation that something will always go wrong. Those who subscribe to this adage are constantly on the lookout, searching for the next shoe to drop. Their conviction is precisely why their prediction comes true. Indeed, a self-fulfilling prophecy.

When you believe you have bad luck, you seek out life experiences that feel like bad luck. If you are always complaining about how unfair life is, certainly the Universe's Search Engine will bring you experiences—return matches—that bolster how right you are. Thinking there are no good women or men left to date, and other patterns of thought with the frequency of lack, are investments today that return those life experiences of tomorrow.

The Universe's Search Engine dutifully searches for and returns frequency matches of what you expect to see. This is quantum physics in action (holding the energy field into what it is you see). What you believe always draws forth evidence as proof of what you believe.

Identify and Dissolve Your B.S.

To recognize belief systems holding you back from achieving your best life be on the lookout for when you hear yourself using words like, "can't," "impossible," and "yeah, but." These are sure signs of blockages holding you back. Also stay attuned to various forms of "That's just how it is," "I know," or "I'm sure this is how it works."

Besides asking "what if" questions to melt away thoughts holding you back, you can ju-jitsu redundant patterns of thought by using the Universe's Search Engine to prove the exact opposite. Shift to the reverse polarity with "I have enough," "I am capable," "I am always taken care of," or "Things are always working out for me," and you will be made right. Your world according to you is caused by you.

Exercising Evolved Thought Consciousness

Since your thoughts are what bring forth your future experiences, and since everything that is must be a thought first, then it follows that we can harness the power of evolved thinking and laws of physics to create future realities according to what we define as important. That's what evolved thought consciousness is.

It's All Here for You

You can have anything you desire. Truly. It's all here for you. Since everything that is was first a thought, it just takes knowing what you want, then bringing yourself into alignment with the vibratory frequencies of those experiences.

COMPLETE EXERCISE 4: EXTREME VISION BOARDING

- Description: Leverage the power of visualization and increase clarity of desire to bring about manifestation quicker.
- Time allocation: 1 hour
- Page 155
- Online: anitamscott.com/ex4 – Password (case sensitive): vision

---

Key Principles

1. Manifestation requires a vibrational match to the vibratory frequency of your desire.

2. There is a trap door where all desires that have *not* manifested reside, held shut by a worn piece of tape ready to break free.

3. Living in the space of already accomplishing your desire emits a powerful bundled thought that moves you into manifestation quicker.

4. During visualization motor neurons fire up as if you were performing the action.

5. Visualization primes the Universe's Search Engine for the delivery of your desires.

6. Vibrational frequencies are things that can be sent, received, and absorbed.

7. Your emissions have the power to impact things.

8. Your brain has transmitter and receiver functionality, able to emit and receive simultaneously.

9. Intention setting is a force of nature, acting like a razor sharp tip on the arrow of your command.

10. To increase the power of your intentions have others hold them for you.

11. The life you have today is directly correlated to your past thoughts.

12. Not accepting your life situation introduces static and brings you more of your current life situation.

13. Make peace with your current life situation by finding the perfection of now.

14. Your first step in deliberate creation is defining what you desire.

15. What can be attracted to you could be better than you can imagine so don't get too specific.

16. Belief systems are thoughts that have become stuck, blocking your ability to see things as they truly are.

17. Self-fulfilling prophecies are caused by belief systems and related emissions.

CHAPTER 5
THE UNIVERSE'S SEARCH ENGINE

"A person is limited only by the thoughts that he chooses."
–James Allen

Discovering that the frequency highway functions like Google is cool, but wait... there's more! This chapter uses recent scientific discoveries to delve deeper into how your thoughts and the Universe's Search Engine join forces to create the quality of your life.

Where Do Your Thoughts Originate?

Let's begin by dissecting how your brain processes thoughts. Between neurons there are gaps. When thoughts fire, synapses positioned at the end of each neuron trigger a chemical signal that floats across the gap to the next neuron. When the chemical signal reaches the neuron on the other side, it converts back into an electrical nerve impulse (similar to how RF waves convert, send, and reassemble). This process has been well studied and documented.

Though not for lack of trying, scientist have yet to discover exactly where in your brain a thought *originates*. When tested with a Magnetic Resonance Imaging (MRI) neurons can be seen firing up, but when all the neurons, synapses, and chemical signals are dissected scientists can never find the thought itself.

Consider then, rather than neurons *instigating* thoughts, what if that firing up is a connection point to something else? Is it possible that thoughts originate from *outside* the brain?

Where Does Your Memory Reside?

One morning I was listening to an intriguing podcast with a scientist whose specific area of interest and concentration was the brain. He set out to locate precisely where memories are stored. After numerous studies performed by him and other scientists, utilizing various technologies to scan the brain—from MRIs, Positron Emission Tomography (PET) and Computed Tomography (CT)—they have yet to identify the part of the brain responsible for storing memories. They can locate connectors and neurons, and similar to thoughts, under study they're able to see neurons firing when someone remembers an event.

However, nowhere to be found is an actual memory containing a smell, sound, or image. These scientists therefore theorized that our memories are stored outside of our brain in something similar to the cloud.[10] The cloud referenced here is related to computer technology that uses the frequency highway to transmit data, which is then stored and can be accessed from anywhere.

The scientist offered the following analogy: Say someone comes to your home to try and figure out what you watched on television last night. They can search for evidence by turning the television on and off and they can check the cables and plugs too, but nowhere to be found is any residual imagery or sound from what you viewed the night before. That's because what you watched didn't come through or reside within the television or cords. The content was transmitted, broadcasted in, and came from outside of these components.

Knowing thoughts move outside of you and are received by the Universe's Search Engine and intended recipients, the theory that thoughts and memories originate and reside in "the cloud" doesn't seem so outlandish.

The Cosmos as a Processor

In another podcast entitled, *Theoretical Physicist Finds Computer Code in String Theory,* Physicist James Gates shared that, while researching fundamental operations of nature, buried deep in pictures of string particles he located a set of equations. The extraordinary thing about these equations is that they exactly match the equations that drive search engines in browsers today.[11]

Wait. What?

You heard right! The fabric of our cosmos is made up of strings of 1s and 0s and is indistinguishable from the computer code that drives the functionality of Google and other search engines.

The Universe's Search Engine

So there is browser computer code within the fabric of the Universe. If that's the case (and it is), the frequency highway as the Universe's Search Engine makes perfect sense. That your thoughts are seen by the Universe's Search Engine as a search command, which then processes that command by retrieving a match that it delivers in the form of a life experience, is by no means a trivial comparison!

IT'S THE WAY THE UNIVERSE IS DESIGNED TO WORK.

Light Speed Processing

It's amazing to think that a Google search takes less than a second to deliver results, despite the fact that more than 40,000 other searches are happening simultaneously. That equates to about 3.5 billion searches per day.

If you think that's remarkable, with a global population of 7.7 billion the Universe's Search Engine processes more than seven billion searches each second. Calculating that everyone emits, say, 70,000 thoughts daily, that's an average of 5.4 trillion searches every day.

Now, the Universe's Search Engine's turnaround time to deliver results is not consistent and fluctuates depending on *frequency alignment*.

How the Universe's Search Engine Functions Like a Browser

As the biggest browser known to man, the Universe's Search Engine functions 24/7/365. It is always on standby, waiting to pick up your input, search for, and return matches.

Here are a few examples of the Universe's Search Engine as a browser in action:

1. **Abundance**
   a. Bundled thoughts: I'm grateful for the roof over my head making me feel joy, love, satisfaction, and gratitude
   b. Universe's Search Engine:
      i. Searches: Look for life experiences matching shelter *bundled* with joy, love, satisfaction, and gratitude.
      ii. Returns: Receive a bonus and move into a nicer home (provided there are no underlying mismatching frequencies).

2. **Lack of Time**
   a. Bundled thoughts: There's never enough time to finish work, homework, or exercise, making me feel overwhelmed, tired, and dejected.
   b. Universe's Search Engine:
      i. Search: Look for life experiences that match lack of time *bundled* with overwhelmed, tired, and dejected.
      ii. Returns: Tasked with a new project at work, and get a teacher who's known for assigning the most amount of homework.

True to its purpose and functionality, the Universe's Search Engine returns matches to your thought emissions.

The Universe's Search Engine Is Neutral

By now you may have surmised that the Universe's Search Engine is completely neutral, and you would be right. It doesn't care if you're a good or bad person. It cannot be influenced by promises or bribes. The Universe's Search Engine doesn't play favorites, skew things in your favor, or vice-versa. It isn't pleased if you're a vegan, or if you volunteer ten hours a week at a local shelter. It's not upset if you yelled at your kids this morning or didn't help that stranger in need. It doesn't judge, reward, or punish.

The Universe's Search Engine is neutral, meaning it does not recognize or categorize anything as positive or negative, and it doesn't work to provide you with good or bad experiences either. The frequency highway brings together matching frequencies and processes requests as you have commanded via your thoughts. There is no amount of wanting, wishing, hoping, or yearning that will make the Universe's Search Engine feel some kind of way. Having those thoughts and feelings only brings you matches of more wanting, wishing, hoping, and yearning. Right?

What does work (according to quantum physics) is pivoting your thoughts to align with the vibrational frequency of what you desire.

You as the Deliberate Co-Creator of Your Life

You prioritize the creation of your life experiences based on:

a) THE AMOUNT OF TIME AND ENERGY YOU SPEND THINKING ABOUT SOMETHING (WHAT YOU'RE BROADCASTING).
b) THE FEELING BUNDLES YOU ATTACH (YOUR MOOD).
c) THE INTENTIONS YOU SET (THE DECISIONS YOU MAKE).

d) WHAT YOU SAY (SOUND WAVES BUNDLES).

e) WHAT YOU DO (YOUR ACTIONS).

The Universe's Search Engine as Your B.F.F.

Even though the Universe's Search Engine is neutral and cultivating a relationship with it would be entirely one-sided, I nevertheless encourage you do just that. Foster an appreciation for its monumental importance in your life and the work it does *for* you day-in and day-out. View it as a tireless partner who slaves all day and night to find and return matches to your search commands—at no charge! Build a relationship based on the limitless potential it offers and affords you.

Deepen the relationship by keeping the Universe's Search Engine pure and clean. Strive for vigilance and only feed it healthy and positive commands. Call it *your* Universe's Search Engine, or best friend forever (BFF). Nickname it "Boomerang" to help remind you that all the thoughts you throw out there will be headed straight back to you in the form of real-life experiences.

Your B.F.F. Has Only Two Jobs

You can count on your new B.F.F. never to fail to perform these two actions:

1. SEARCHING FOR AND RETURNING MATCHES TO THE VIBRATORY FREQUENCY OF YOUR BUNDLED THOUGHTS.

2. MAKING YOU RIGHT. (IF YOU SAY, "I'M SO TIRED ALL OF THE TIME!" THE UNIVERSE'S SEARCH ENGINE WILL CONTINUE TO PROVIDE EXHAUSTING EXPERIENCES AND SITUATIONS).

Key Principles

1. Buried within string particle that makes up the fabric of the cosmos is computer code matching exactly the code that drives search engines.
2. The Universe's Search Engine is simply an electric processer, processing your thoughts as orders.
3. The Universe's Search Engine is completely neutral. It doesn't care how kind, mean, deserving, or desperate you are.
4. The Universe's Search Engine is perfectly perfect at its job, never failing to find and bring you matches, and make you right.

CHAPTER 6
SELF-AWARENESS MATTERS

"Unless you make the unconscious conscious, it will
direct your life and you will call it fate."
–C.G. Jung

With a firm understanding of how real-life experiences are created by your emissions from firing neurons, nothing is more important than the quality of your thoughts. To facilitate your ability to harness the power of thought to the fullest we delve into expanding thought consciousness through self-awareness.

How to Achieve Self-Awareness

Self-awareness is a crucial ingredient in creating the life you want, because successfully shifting thoughts requires that you first become aware of them. Sigmund Freud, Austrian neurologist and founder of psychoanalysis, compared the mind to an iceberg. He theorized that what you're currently aware of is the tip of the iceberg at less than 15%, with the majority and most important part of the mind lying below the surface.[11] More recently *US News and World Report* journalist and author Marianne Szegedy-Maszak has come to the conclusion that, "According to cognitive neuroscientists, we are conscious of only about 5% of our cognitive activity, so most of our decisions, actions, emotions, and behavior depends on the 95% of brain activity that goes beyond our conscious awareness."[12]

To be clear, 100% of your thoughts are broadcasting. What both Freud and Szegedy-Masza are saying is the vast majority of what you're thinking about goes completely unnoticed by you! The good news is the unconscious mind can easily be brought to consciousness[13] by growing self-awareness.

Growing an awareness practice gives you the ability to uncover, curtail, and manage your thoughts rather than letting them "direct your life and ... call it fate," per Carl Jung.

The best tools proven to build awareness are mindfulness and meditation.

Mindfulness

Being mindful is a mental state where you are fully present, living in the moment, tuned into your thoughts and how you feel on an emotional and physical level. Mindfulness gained a lot of traction in the 90s with Eckhart Tolle's book, *The Power of Now*, which celebrated the art of being present.

Here are a couple of practical examples of what mindfulness looks like during everyday activities:

1. As you walk, pay attention to feeling your feet beneath you, along with the swing of your legs and arms. Listen for the birds chirping and count how many different tweets you hear. Observe the crack in the sidewalk where a beautiful flower has emerged and experience wonderment at how it found its way there to raise its head high against all odds. Appreciate the blossom's effort, beauty and poise.

2. During dinner fully enjoy the aroma, rich color and flavor of your vegetables. Consider where they came from, who planted and tended to them, the amount of water they drank and how the

rays of the sun found their way onto its leaves. Give thanks to the plant for its nutrition, for the caretakers and to those who picked, packaged and transported them.

Take these two serene examples and now juxtapose them with taking a walk while on your cell phone and crushing the flower beneath your foot, oblivious of its existence. Or with scarfing down the vegetables while watching television, barely noticing their vibrant color and taste. Can you feel the difference in the energy surrounding the mindful exercises versus the mind-*less*?

Here's a serious question: When was the last time you were in the shower with yourself? When you're in the shower most likely you're thinking about work, kids, vacation, who said what to who, or what you need to do today. The next time you take a shower press pause on this barrage of thoughts and practice a moment of mindfulness by feeling the water hitting your skin, appreciating the lathering soap as it makes bubbles on your body, and hearing the running water. Do your best to keep your thoughts in the shower with you.

Mindfulness Is Your New M.O.

Your goal is to make living mindfully your standard state of being. It's a new approach to life where you're no longer on autopilot. And it is one that will make you much happier and healthier!

Give it a quick try. In this moment, feel the sensation of the seat that's beneath you providing comfort and support. Feel the weight of your arms and your legs. That's it. You did it! You created a mini-moment of mindfulness. The more you practice the easier and more natural it becomes and the more your awareness muscle grows.

As you progress through your day aim to be mindful on at least three occasions. Besides moving you into the present, it interrupts the pattern of incessant thoughts and makes space for clarity.

Mindfulness also induces a mindset of gratitude, which is a great frequency to have boomeranging back to you!

Meditation

We turn now to the other highly effective self-awareness tool: meditation. Meditation is agnostic, so you can have a religion and practice meditation too. Besides increasing awareness, the scientific benefits of meditation are well-studied and documented across health, social life, self-control, happiness, productivity, and wisdom. Who doesn't want that? Meditation has the absolute power to transform your mind, bring about a deep state of serenity, and substantially increase self-awareness.[14]

The Answers Lie in the Spaces

The beauty of meditation is that it provides your mind the necessary space to become aware of your thoughts, and expands your ability to separate yourself from your conditioned thoughts. The practice positions you as an observer of your mind, like you're pulling up a chair to a picture glass window to watch your thoughts as they parade in and out.

In addition to making room for thought-observation, meditation makes space for input too. To demonstrate how that works imagine a jar filled halfway with dirt. What happens when fresh clean water rushes in? The water stirs up the dirt, lifting it out until eventually the water is clean. This is how meditation works. It moves out the old silt and cleanses your mind, making room for thought observation and divine inspiration.

Given the average person has a new thought every 1.2 seconds, hitting pause for even just one minute can strike fifty thoughts from occurring.

Flip from Transmitter to Receiver

Have you ever heard the saying: Sometimes you need to slow down in order to speed up? You may have experienced this when you stepped away from a problem because you couldn't figure it out, only to find an hour later or when you woke up the next morning you had the answer.

Giving your thoughts a timeout by releasing them introduces a break that leads to clarity. Think of it this way: When you're thinking 100% of the time your brain is 100% occupied, so you leave no room for input. Moving into stillness flips your switch from transmitter to receiver, facilitating access to insights and downloads that are always available to you but aren't possible to tune into when you're constantly emanating thoughts.

Where to Start

Whether you have practiced meditation before or have never tried it, simply start where you are. Begin with fifteen seconds and grow that to one minute, then add more and more time as you progress. Ideally your practice will build to meditating between fifteen to twenty minutes each day.

What to Expect When You're Expecting (to Meditate)

Before trying to meditate here's a heads up of what you can expect:

- **Monkey mind:** It's completely normal to experience thoughts parading in and out. As you become aware that you're "thinking" rather than focusing on your breath, simply acknowledge the thoughts with a "Hello there" before gently pushing them aside and moving your focus back to your breath.
- **Itching**: There it is on the tip of your nose, your right toe, your left armpit, wherever. Instead of jumping to scratch an itch wait to see if it'll subside. If it doesn't dissipate it's okay to give a scratch, but know that your monkey mind likes to

distract you so see if you can move past it by returning your focus back to your breath.

- **Noise**: There goes the crop-duster, the doorbell, the neighbor's dogs, or the hotrod. Simply acknowledge noises as they arise and then let them roll off. What works for me in the first few minutes of my meditation is to actively listen for as many noises as I can hear, labeling them and appreciating the different sounds. Then I let them gently dissipate.
- **Self-judgment:** Saying, "I'm not doing this right" stops you so be patient, kind and gentle with yourself. Start with fifteen seconds of focused breathing and congratulate yourself when you've accomplished that. From there, set a goal of thirty seconds, and so on. Like a newbie at the gym, you'll need practice to grow this muscle.
- **Find the right place:** Be sure you practice meditation in a comfortable and quiet location where you won't be disturbed. If you believe there is a chance that you will be bothered, you won't be able to fully relax as you anticipate an interruption.

Form Basics

You can meditate sitting or lying down (note if you lie down the chance you'll fall asleep increases exponentially). Your eyes can be closed or open but not focused on anything. Place your hands palms up on your lap if you're sitting. If you're lying down, lay your arms alongside your body. You can touch the tip of your index fingers to the tips of your thumbs if you like, and then begin breathing in and out through your nose.

Meditation Types

There are hundreds (if not more) ways to meditate, with the majority usually starting by settling and silencing yourself, then becoming aware of your breath for the first few minutes. Transitioning into stillness by quieting your mind and body prepares you to move from transmitter to receiver.

Here are two simple meditations to try once you're in the space and position outlined in the prior paragraphs:

1. **Breath Meditation:**

    a. For a count of four: Focus on your breath and inhale.
    b. For a count of four: Hold that breath.
    c. For a count of four: Exhale.
    d. For a count of four: Hold again.
    e. Loop back to step a. and continue this pattern.

Feel free to modify this meditation by either changing the count or not holding your breath in between. It really doesn't matter. The objective is to move your thoughts to your breath and keep your thoughts there.

2. **Conscious Breathing:**

Thanks to our body's autonomic nervous system, breathing takes place automatically all day, every day without any interference from you. In this meditation your objective is to bear witness to this by simply observing your breath rather than trying to control or manage it.

Once you're settled and in stillness there is nothing to do other than observe the air flowing in through your nostrils, down your throat and filling your lungs. When you're in the space of observing your breath notice: How deep into your lungs does the air travel? How far does your chest expand and contract with each inhale and exhale? Are your lungs automatically drawing in the air, or is your breath originating from within your nostrils? This observation will create space and foster well-being.

Note that meditation is a mindfulness technique too. Since you're unable to have more than one thought at a time, when you're focusing on your breath you're unable to think about anything else.

Both practices immediately move you into the present moment, so thoughts about what happened yesterday or what may happen tomorrow subside.

Monkey Mind

Even though meditating sounds and is simple, don't expect it to be easy. It takes practiced effort to curtail the plethora of thoughts running through your head. Though monkey mind was briefly mentioned, it's worthy of further discussion since it's the biggest challenge and deterrent for those attempting to meditate.

Not if, but *when* you find that your mind won't settle down it's helpful to know that it's not just you. More than 2500 years ago Buddha described the human mind as filled with drunken monkeys, jumping, screeching, chattering, and endlessly carrying on.[15]

Monkey Taming

Recalling the quantum physics law of least resistance, avoid trying to do the impossible and completely silence your thoughts. Instead, your goal is to *tame* the monkeys and have them grow more peaceful over time.

Meditation fosters your ability to decrease the barrage of thoughts and manage your monkeys, observing and separating yourself from them. As your awareness muscle strengthens, the monkeys will no longer be in control. You will no longer be a slave to your thoughts, which gives you the ability to choose thoughts in harmony and alignment with your desires.

Always take the approach of bringing your thoughts into submission by acknowledging them. Then lovingly brush them away and return your focus back to your breath. I find it helpful to imagine a babbling brook next to me during meditations. I simply brush thoughts into it as I become aware of them, to gently float away.

Growing Your Awareness Muscle Feels Like...

The following potty training analogy resembles what growing your self-awareness muscle feels like. As a newborn baby, unbeknownst to you, urine collected in your bladder and was then released into a diaper several times throughout the day. Completely oblivious of the muscles controlling this bodily function, when potty training began it required tremendous focus and effort to learn the many subtleties of bladder control. With practice, however, you became more and more familiar with the sensations and signals, until finally the process required the tiniest of focus. Today you use the bathroom by rote. It requires little to no focus.

It's much the same with growing your self-awareness where, in the beginning you have no cognition that bundled thoughts are spilling out of you. When you become aware of these continuous emissions it takes focused effort to recognize the sensations that signal what you're emitting. With practice your muscle grows and soon self-awareness becomes your natural state of being.

When and Where

Mindfulness and meditation help raise your vibration and release resistance. And the beauty is they can be practiced anywhere. During hectic days in the office I used a portion of my bathroom break to observe my breath. Just a couple of minutes of conscious breathing brought peace and fostered clarity.

Level of Effort

Many people have a difficult time believing or conceptualizing that their thoughts are responsible for creating the lives they have today, mostly because the whole process is invisible. Often the intangibility makes the laws of science and physics difficult to comprehend and buy into. As visual beings we are far better at understanding and trusting in things we can see and touch.

There's also a resistance to putting forth the effort necessary to manage your thoughts. If this applies to you, before dismissing this path let's compare the energy it takes to live life as a *deliberate creator* versus ignoring these universal principles and living life as a *passive reactor*:

INPUT: EXPENDED ENERGY	
DELIBERATE CREATOR	**PASSIVE REACTOR**
Practice mindfulness	Experience frustration with what is
Practice meditation	Practice a frantic pace of life
Choose high vibratory thoughts	Reminisce about bygone situations
Practice positive visualization	Worry about what may come to pass
Practice self-love	Self-judgment and blame
Follow the path of least resistance	Resist what is

Now compare the life experiences the Universe's Search Engine returns from those broadcasted thoughts:

OUTPUT: LIFE EXPERIENCES	
DELIBERATE CO-CREATOR	**PASSIVE REACTOR**
Experience clarity of thought	More frustration with what is
Enjoy space, guidance, and knowing	Exhaustion and frustration
Surrounded by high vibratory situations	Continuously relive situations
Universe's Search Engine primed so desires are delivered quickly	Suffer in worry and bring about what you're worrying about
Live in alignment and good health	Disharmony brings dis-ease
Reduced resistance brings increased flow and peace	Get more of what you've resisted

While it's true streaming thoughts willy-nilly is easier because no effort is needed, sloppy thinking and putting out habitual brushfires requires much more time and energy in the long run. Big picture: Deliberate creators expend much less energy because there's less negativity and drama. There are fewer fires to put out. Plus, the payoff for your proactive effort is getting all you desire, which inevitably leads to a far happier, healthier, more fulfilled life.

As depicted in the potty training analogy, it takes focused effort on the front end to become a deliberate creator. But, over time, new patterns of thought are established. Eventually, living life as a deliberate creator becomes your natural way of being. It's never too late to start! The more you practice, the easier it becomes.

Let the Light Shine in

It takes at least five positive statements to erase a single negative one[30] so it's useful to uncover what's going on beneath the surface in order to curtail undermining thoughts. While working on cultivating self-awareness a client once asked, "How can I balance being self-aware with self-doubt?" As her self-awareness grew, she unexpectedly uncovered harsh and critical self-talk.

Growing her self-awareness did not cause her self-doubt. Rather, it provided a window into her subconscious thoughts that had been running amuck behind the scenes unchecked all along. Without practicing self-awareness that self-judgment and doubt would have continued to who-knows-what detriment. Surely, it was limiting and minimizing her potentiality as all harsh and critical self-talk does. What she experienced is exactly what you want to happen.

Starting an awareness practice pulls back the blinds to shine a bright light on self-talk, illuminating the 95% of thoughts that are hidden away in your unconscious mind. Since, subconsciously or not, every thought fires neurons and those emanating thoughts are transmitted, awareness provides you with an opportunity to acknowledge and shift thoughts, thus giving you the power to design a life of unbridled happiness and abundance.

Bridge to Connections

We will delve into metaphysics in Chapter 8, but it is relevant to mention here that meditation acts like a bridge to the metaphysical. It's a tool capable of adjusting your vibration and connecting you with other levels of consciousness and energetic beings.

Create an intention to establish, cultivate, and nurture these relationships to gain access to the wisdom, knowing, guidance, and synchro-destiny where the stars seem to align.

Key Principles

1. Becoming a co-creator requires awareness of the thoughts you emanate.
2. 95% of your thoughts are subconscious.
3. Self-awareness is a muscle that must be cultivated and grown.
4. Mindfulness and meditation are tools that facilitate self-awareness, raising your vibration, releasing resistance, thought observation, connections, and space.
5. When you're exuding thoughts 100% of the time there's no space to observe and receive.
6. Monkey mind is normal and to be expected.
7. Your goal isn't to silence all thoughts, but to tame them over time so you're no longer a slave to them.
8. Becoming a deliberate co-creator requires an investment of time, but in the long run less effort is required and the payoff is a happier life.
9. Creating space shines a light on your self-talk.

CHAPTER 7
MIND MATTERS

"The quality of our life depends on the quality of our mind."
–Sri Sri Ravi Shankar

To increase the quality of your emissions this chapter will provide further insights into how your brain works, along with additional tools to help better manage what's on your mind.

Thoughts Reshape Your Brain

Remember, when thoughts fire, chemical signals float from one synapse (positioned at the end of neurons) to another. In his article, "The Science of Happiness: Why Complaining Is Literally Killing You," futurist and techno-optimist Steven Parton says, "Every time (an) electrical charge is triggered, the synapses grow closer together in order to decrease the distance the electrical charge has to cross. The brain is rewiring its own circuitry, physically changing itself, to make it easier and more likely that the proper synapses will share the chemical link and thus spark together—in essence, making it easier for the thought to trigger. Therefore … your thoughts reshape your brain."[16]

Parton continues. "… the synapses you've most strongly bonded together (by thinking about more frequently) come to represent your default personality… and most easily accessible thoughts."

In other words, the more you think about something the more you create a pathway in your brain for it. Similarly, walking through tall grass for the first time may not disturb the landscape. However, continually walking across the same path lends itself to creating a thoroughfare. The difference and danger is repetitive thoughts create neural pathways, like highway shortcuts or deep links, auto-routing you to think the same thoughts over and over again.

Mirror Neurons

In Chapter 2 we learned that firing neurons emit electromagnetic waves, but there's still more to uncover about the power and implications of firing neurons. Neuroscientist Vilayanur Ramachandran discovered that *mirror neurons* fire when you watch someone else do something. For instance, watching somebody bounce a ball triggers your mirror neurons as if *you* are bouncing the ball.[17]

The significance of this discovery cannot be overstated. It holds true for everything you observe, regardless of whether you're seeing it in person or not. As you watch anything (including movies or television) neurons light up as if you are performing the action, or as if the activity is happening to you.

Funnel into Your Brain

Building on our understanding that firing neurons emit electromagnetic waves, this revelation tells us that when you're binge watching your favorite Netflix series (assuming you're in veg-mode and only receiving input) you are emitting thoughts in tandem since your brain processes everything you see.

It would be accurate then to imagine a funnel at the top of your head pouring everything you see into your brain for processing. Thoughts—regardless of where they originate—are picked up by your devoted B.F.F. nonstop to search for and return matches according to what it receives.

No Exclusion of Thought

There is no off switch for your brain. Everything you take in creates sparks, resulting in broadcasted thoughts.

As a binary processor, the Universe's Search Engine doesn't have an off switch either, nor the capacity to distinguish a point of origin. Consistently neutral, the Universe's Search Engine doesn't know or care where thoughts or actions originate. It simply receives *all* thoughts, searches for frequency matches, and returns real-life experiences.

Protect Your Airspace

Oprah Winfrey, an avid proponent of the concept of the Law of Attraction and power of positive thinking, and who was critical to these concepts becoming mainstream, is extremely selective with what she listens to, reads, and watches to guard what comes in, and in turn what goes out, to the Universe's Search Engine. She even requests her drivers turn the radio off when she gets into a chauffeured car. It makes perfect sense to monitor and take great care with what you take in.

COMPLETE EXERCISE 5: THOUGHT DIAGNOSTIC

- Description: Uncover what you're consciously and unconsciously broadcasting.
- Time allocation: 1 hour
- Page 157
- Online: anitamscott.com/ex5 — Password (case sensitive): thought

---

Selective Ignorance

Another tool at your disposal to increase the quality of your thought emissions is selective ignorance. When you make a decision to spend zero time thinking, learning, or hearing about a particular subject it renders you ignorant on that topic. Logically, you can't know everything. There's simply too much to know. Trying to do so would be like going to a bookstore or library and attempting to read every book they have.

Since brain space is limited to a finite number of thoughts, institute selective ignorance by choosing what's important to you, what you have a desire and ability to influence, and what to eliminate.

As an admitted energy snob I apply selective ignorance in my day-to-day life to protect my airspace and precious time in the following ways:

- Record all television shows so I can zoom through commercials.
- Don't watch particular political shows.

Positive Psychology

Since thoughts are valuable things that transform into your quality life, it's helpful to talk about your demeanor in relation to the way you approach the world.

There have been a number of studies that seek to understand what distinguishes a lucky person from an unlucky one. In 2006, scientist Richard Wiseman assembled two groups of people—one group believed they were lucky, and the other believed they were unlucky. He asked them to look through a newspaper and count how many pictures were inserted.

Individuals in the self-proclaimed "lucky" group were much more likely to notice that on the second page of the paper there was a half-page ad that read in big bold letters "STOP COUNTING." Just underneath these words the number of pictures within the paper was provided. What was different about these lucky folks was the *expectation* of things going their way, so they were always on the lookout for opportunities.[18]

The study concluded that being lucky is a mindset. It's having a disposition of an expectation that opportunities are on the way, always. When you expect opportunities you are brought matches of opportunities. People who consider themselves lucky only differ from others because they are keen at using the quantum physics Law of Attraction. They are continuously sending the Universe's Search Engine positive thoughts, like "things always go my way" and "things come easily to me." And so they do!

External Versus Internal

What's your viewpoint on self-worth? How do you determine your value? Is it your performance at work, or how much money you make? Is it how many likes you get on Instagram or Facebook, how much you donate, or help others? Is it how many vacations you take, books you publish, pounds you lose, or friends you have?

Self-esteem issues and lack of self-confidence are often caused by deriving worth from the outside and basing it on what others think. When your value is obtained externally you are always seeking approval, ultimately allowing others to have authority over your happiness. This will always leave you disappointed because you're being judged by someone else's standards and value systems, which are based on their whims and personal definitions of importance.

Extracting your value in this way is a difficult and unhealthy way to live. Liken it to a flower with shallow roots spread across rocks, reaching out desperately for moisture and nourishment. There's exposure and higher risk of malnutrition and damage, which renders you weak.

In contrast, obtaining your value and self-esteem internally is akin to a flower with roots deeply embedded in the ground, where there's an abundance of nutrient-rich soil. You are balanced, firmly rooted in who you are and what you stand for. If a storm comes and the wind rages, you aren't swayed or injured too deeply if at all.

In order to achieve sustained happiness, your self-worth and value must come from your own value system made up of what you consider to be good. If you're not sure what that looks like, get comfortable and create space through mindfulness and meditation to tune in and listen for the answers.

Don't Scapegoat Negative Feelings

You are the most perfect version of you. This includes having positive and negative feelings. Both are important and serve a purpose. For instance, fear alerts you to danger, guilt stops you from doing things you shouldn't do, and anger motivates you to take action. Negative feelings also provide contrast, casting a light on what's important to you to help you determine preferences.

Remember your moods are like a GPS, where feelings indicate what you're thinking about. As you become aware of negative emotions jiu-jitsu that energy into something positive. The key is to not sit and marinate in the negative. Besides emitting those transmissions, wallowing in negativity "has seriously terrible consequences for your mental and physical health."[19]

Rote as a Gold Mine

Rote is the use of memory with little intelligence. It's when your brain is on autopilot which occurs when performing repetitious activities like doing the dishes, taking a shower, brushing your teeth, and even driving. For example, when you're on the highway and can't remember how a car got in front of you, you were in rote. Rote time is included in the mix of 95% of your thoughts being subconscious, and as such can be seen as a gold mine that you can tap into to become more conscious of what's on your mind, and more deliberate about what you choose to think about.

PART A: NEGATIVE MIND MATTERS

To expedite shifts away from low vibrational patterns of thoughts we must dig into negative behaviors and patterns that may be holding you back from achieving your best life.

Complaining Infects Others

Complaining is a verbal statement of non-acceptance. Dissatisfaction and frustration with what is, flies in the face of the law of least resistance. Bundled onto those low vibratory thoughts are sound waves that not only increase intensity, they also produce negative ions that attach to you and the listener. Yes, complaining is a virus that dirties the airwaves and infects others! Even more detrimental, complaining has the potential to kill you. In "The Science of Happiness" Steven Parton goes on to explain, "When your brain is firing off these synapses of anger, you're weakening your immune system; you're raising your blood pressure, increasing your risk of heart disease, obesity and diabetes, and a plethora of other ailments."

If that's not enough to make you think twice about complaining, there's more. Complaining rewires your brain for negativity, which explains why complainers always complain. Finally, but importantly, when you complain you're making a choice to squander your time given there is a finite amount and nothing productive comes from it.

When you catch yourself complaining switch to acknowledging your dissatisfaction, then immediately to solutioning, asking, "What can I *do* about this situation in a healthy and constructive manner?" That's all that's needed to flip your emanating thoughts from negative to positive leaving you and those around you happier and healthier.

The Past

Any time you find yourself thinking about the past you're not living in the present. Since you no longer have yesterday—it's truly gone and passed—spending your limited brainpower reminiscing wastes precious energy.

Consider again those Olympic athletes who visualized their races resulting in motor neurons firing as if they were physically running a race. When you think about the past you are exercising visualization, with motor neurons firing as if you are living it now. The Universe's Search Engine cannot tell the difference between your memory and a new experience so those firing neurons emanate thoughts regardless.

Stuck in a Groove

If it seems like nothing's ever changing for you or others, what's really going on is repetitive thoughts are returning repetitive experiences. A sure sign of being stuck in a groove is when you say or hear the phrase, "Why is this always happening to me?" According to Dr. Joe Dispenza, researcher, educator, and author of *Evolve Your Brain, You Are The Placebo* and other books on brain science, 90% of your thoughts are the same thoughts you had the day before which is why the Universe's Search Engine is returning 90% of the same experiences giving the appearance that nothing's ever changing!

Parton's explanation about repetitive thoughts reshaping your brain, causing you to continuously replay the same thoughts, is precisely why 90% of your thoughts are the same as the day before. This research illustrates the colloquialism "habits of thought."

For my techies, imagine buying a software package with every single video game ever created. When you bring it home it's full of potentiality. You could go here and play this or go there and play that—whatever your heart desires! But not too long afterwards a glitch shows up that progressively impedes access to games until eventually you're only able to play one game, the same game, over and over again. In this analogy the software represents your brain, which starts out as a clean slate. The glitch symbolizes belief systems and habits of thought acquired over time that have turned into a solid, locking you into living the same experiences over and over again, ultimately stifling your life experience.

Given deep crevasses in your brain cause you to continually think the same thoughts, producing a repetitive loop, trying to stop thinking these engrained thoughts will be next to impossible. Rather than resisting those thoughts, choose to think different thoughts altogether. You can also leverage meditation and mindfulness to introduce space and disrupt patterns of thought.

COMPLETE EXERCISE 6: CATCH AND RELEASE

- Description: Identify programmed thoughts and foster new neural pathways.
- Time allocation: 25 minutes
- Page 160
- Online: anitamscott.com/ex6 — Password (case sensitive): release

---

Regret

Regret and wishing something did or didn't happen doesn't change a thing. Therefore, logically, regret is a complete waste of time. Furthermore, it actually compounds your suffering. You felt bad when the incident occurred, and you continue to suffer with remorse. The vibratory frequency of regret is very low so it's an effective blocker of the many positives in store for you.

To move past thoughts of mistakes and regret, look at the event as refining you, not defining you. Determine the takeaways by way of silver lining or contrast to help you to get clear about what you do want. Tease out the lessons, and any time you find yourself back in regret flip the script by acknowledging and being grateful for the expansion and clarity of desire.

Judgment and Blame

If you find yourself in the space of judgment and blame, take proponent of alternative-medicine and prominent New Age philosopher Deepak Chopra's guidance to heart to, "Do your best to realize that everyone is doing their best from their state of consciousness. Have the intention to forgive others and yourself for any trespasses that may have resulted in pain."[20]

He also says, "When you think that someone has wronged you, you make yourself superior to them by judging, placing blame, and believing in your rightness and the belief that you need to forgive them." That's a whole lot of negative energy being expelled.

Consider this perfect metaphor. It's not the snakebite that kills you, it's the venom. In other words, it's not the incident, but your continual regurgitating of the incident that poisons you. With this in mind, instead of hanging around in judgment and blame, practice forgiveness to release the venom and free yourself in order to increase the frequency of your vibes.

Worry

Worry lives in the past *and* future, so when you spend time worrying you're unable to live in the present. Plus, when you worry you suffer twice. Worrying about "what might be" is the first pain, and if what you've worried about comes to bear there's a second suffering.

Recall self-fulfilling prophecies. When you worry you are choosing a lane that's linked to what it is you're worrying about, and therefore drawing forth the return of it. To stop that momentum, switch tracks and think about anything that brings you joy.

Anger

When you sit in anger due to something being unjust and unfair you've made a decision to feed the Universe's Search Engine a command to find a match of anger and resentment, so be on the lookout for more of that. Your anger compounds and doubles down with the law of least resistance, even when you're completely in the right.

To loosen that up, acknowledge your anger then move forward utilizing your emotional energy in a more constructive manner. Play a game of "find the gift" to identify the silver lining, or imagine how someone you admire would have handled the situation.

COMPLETE EXERCISE 7: PERCEPTION SHIFTER

- Description: Expand perspectives to view scenarios from another lens.
- Time allocation: 25 minutes
- Page 162
- Online: anitamscott.com/ex7 — Password (case sensitive): shift

---

Fear

Fear is a huge enabler that loves to keep you small, giving you plenty of reasons why you can't or shouldn't do something. More often than not, fear is based on fiction not fact, and comes from an engrained belief system that the world is a scary place, or life is unsafe. When this pattern of thought has been programmed during your childhood, it's the way you operate in the world. Likely fear is always creeping into your thoughts on an unconscious level. Of course, fearful thoughts create experiences that warrant fear courtesy of the Universe's Search Engine.

Hiding behind your fear actually makes the fear bigger, too. To minimize fear, seek to understand if there's any validity. When related to physical safety it's wise to take heed, but when it's related to keeping you in your lane—your comfort zone—then your opportunity is to stretch and overcome it. Put effort into trying to do or accept something you normally wouldn't. Give "yes" a try rather than clinging to "no," and watch as synchro-destiny arrives underneath your leap of faith to gracefully support and guide you. Fear can be neutralized by listening, acknowledging and thanking it, then considering the possibilities of moving into trust.

Revenge

Have you heard the saying, "Revenge is a poison meant for others which you end up swallowing"? The emotion associated with revenge produces an extremely low vibrational frequency that, not only robs you of joy in your life, it is also likely to make you sick. Exercise forgiveness, not for the other person's sake, but for your own health, sanity, and quality of life.

REDO EXERCISE 6: CATCH AND RELEASE

- Description: Work through heartache, regret, disappointment, failure, grudges and resentment, shifting momentum and creating new neural pathways.
- Time allocation: 25 minutes
- Page 160
- Online: anitamscott.com/ex6 – Password (case sensitive): release

---

Ask: What Am I Going to Do About It?

While it may sound and feel counter-intuitive, since what you resist persists, try moving into the space of your worry, fear, anger, and other negative emotions. Since breaking something shatters it, leaving behind jagged little pieces, bestselling author Louise Hay, who founded Hay House and is considered one of the founders of the self-help movement, guides that you don't want to *break* the habit of living in these feelings. Instead, your goal is to *dissolve* the feeling so it disappears altogether. Do this by lovingly acknowledging your feelings, then asking what you can do about a situation. Knowing full well that thoughts have power, move into self-resolution, allowing, trust, and faith, and envision a positive outcome.

Self-help author and motivational speaker Dr. Wayne Dyer shared that even when you know you are 100% right about something, if you find yourself arguing or getting mad trying to convince others of your rightness, then it's in your best interest to stop and change your thoughts to something more pleasant. Why would he say that? Because he knew that frustration and anger emit low frequency bundled thoughts that return negative life experiences.

When Dr. Dyer spoke about food manufactures using GMOs that were poisoning the ocean he couldn't let go of the fight, and he would belabor the wrongness. Boy would he get mad! He received guidance to turn that frustration into a pleasurable feeling so as not to be emitting negative frequency vibrations through his direct resistance. Shifting his thoughts to what he *could* do, Dr. Dyer joined a local coalition that effectively influenced lawmakers to ban the use of GMOs in his area. What a great example of pivoting anger into passion by asking, "What can I do to help the situation?"

This example showcases how negative emotions can motivate you to change things you don't like or approve of. Asking and then answering the simple question "What am I going to do about it?" has the power to change everything.

Affirmations

We move away from minimizers to end this chapter on a high note, leaving you with one more tool for your arsenal that does a phenomenal job of shifting and dissolving negative thoughts and belief systems: Affirmations.

Affirmations are positive declarations that work to reprogram your brain, melt away limiting belief systems, and improve self-confidence. They have the power to restructure your brain by interrupting patterns and bypassing the worn-in grooves made by repetitive negative thoughts, replacing them with new, healthier neural pathways.

Affirmations rock the needle out of the grove so you can stop playing the same old record and start dancing to a new beat. They are liberating! Here are a few examples of some popular ones:

- EVERYTHING IS ALWAYS WORKING OUT FOR ME
- I LOVE AND APPROVE OF MYSELF
- I AM THE ARCHITECT OF MY LIFE
- I HAVE ENOUGH
- I AM ENOUGH
- I AM WORTHY OF ALL GOOD THINGS
- NO ONE'S ABOVE ME. NO ONE'S BELOW ME. I AM EQUAL TO ALL.
- I AM SAFE
- I AM LOVED
- I TRUST MYSELF
- MY LIFE IS JUST BEGINNING

Lastly, the ever-popular limiting belief system of "I can't" can be rerouted by repeating the affirmation "I am capable" or "I can and I will."

I offer this important caveat: When choosing affirmations be certain you feel the truth behind the words. Besides changing the frequency when you practice an affirmation that you don't completely believe, that questioning, doubt or disbelief can also work to affirm patterns of thought holding you back instead of dissolving them.

Key Principles

1. When you see someone do something your neurons fire as if you were doing it.

2. When you watch television or a movie, that content funnels into your brain and processes as if the actions are happening to you or you are performing the actions.
3. The Universe's Search Engine can't distinguish where a thought originates and takes what you emanate as your commands.
4. There isn't such a thing as lucky people, only people that have an expectation that things always go their way.
5. Feelings are a direct result of your thoughts.
6. Negative emotions are gifts alerting you to your thoughts, motivating you to make changes, and helping you to get clear on preferences.
7. Self-worth and value must come from your own value system made up of what's important to you.
8. Repetitive thoughts reshape your brain making it easier to think those same thoughts.
9. 90% of your thoughts are the same from the day before, therefore returning 90% of the same experiences and giving the appearance that nothing's ever changing.
10. Shift negative vibes associated with heartache, regret, disappointment, failure, grudges and resentment by considering and identifying the lessons.
11. Affirmations are powerful in rerouting neural pathways and changing limiting beliefs.

PART II:
OTHER COMPONENTS

This section overlays the principles presented in Part I with other important components influencing your quality of life so you can actively harness all avenues in order to live your very best life.

CHAPTER 8
METAPHYSICS MATTERS

"Spirituality does not come from religion. It comes from our soul."
–Anthony Douglas Williams

The Universe's Search Engine and bundled thoughts are only part of the equation delivering your life experiences. There's another component at play readying and delivering how your life unfolds: The metaphysical component.

Since metaphysics diverges from known, proven science as demonstrated in Part One, Part Two takes a leap of faith, introducing concepts and assertions based on studies across hundreds of years. I encourage you to gravitate towards what resonates and leave behind what does not.

Merriam-Webster.com's "Did You Know?" feature says of metaphysics, "Just as physics deals with the laws that govern the physical world (such as those of gravity or the properties of waves), metaphysics describes what is beyond physics—the nature and origin of reality itself, the immortal soul, and the existence of a supreme being."[21]

The metaphysical component is agnostic and simply the concern or interest in things other than material and physical. Almost everyone believes in something greater than themselves. Source, supreme consciousness, One, God, Allah, all knowing, Holy Spirit,

Deva, infinite intelligence, angels, guides and energy force are just a few of the terms associated to invisible energies.

You Are a Soul

Diving right in: You are not your body. To illustrate the difference between your body and soul, recall the earlier story where scientists theorized memories are stored outside of your brain in a cloud, using the example of searching for content within the television, cables, and plugs and finding none. Without content streaming into it, the television is rendered little more than a ginormous paperweight. The same applies to the way your soul, a non-physical consciousness inhabiting your body, brings forth non-physical characteristics like your personality and sense of humor. Those attributes don't come from your body; they come from your soul. You are a soul in a human form, having a physical experience. An analogy for my techies: You in this carnation are the peripheral; Your inner being is the docking station.

If you've ever witnessed someone pass away, you have a pretty good sense of this ringing true. When a couple of my loved ones were on their deathbed it was hard to pry me away. Yet at the moment of their transition I was overcome with an overwhelming compulsion to leave the room as quickly as possible. There was a crystal clear line of demarcation from us being together, to me being alone. Instantaneously their bodies transitioned into empty shells; it was unmistakable that they were "gone."

It's no coincidence that most if not all religions and spiritual groups believe in the eternity of souls and consciousness beyond the body. Existence as a non-physical soul, then moving into human form, then returning to spirit form isn't a new or radical concept.

As pure energy your immortal soul existed prior to this incarnation and continues living after your body dies.

Inner Being Has All Prior Knowledge

Since your soul was alive before this incarnation and lives on after your body dies it's easier to fathom that you have experienced *many* lives and this lifetime is only a portion of who you are. Your inner being (aka inner self, inner wisdom, innermost being, or true self) is the part of you that remains non-physical and connected to Source. It has all prior knowledge and wisdom from all lifetimes and is therefore a powerful source of intelligence.

Spiritual Amnesia

So why don't you remember your incarnations? Typically you come into each lifetime with no memory of prior lives due to what's known as spiritual amnesia. This gift of forgetfulness provides a veil from who you were in past lives, making it easier to fully integrate into this lifetime.

If you or someone you know has ever said, "I don't know why I'm like this, I just am and always have been," there's a strong likelihood that statement is related to carrying over a sense, feeling, or behavior from a previous lifetime (perhaps due to quantum entanglement).

Past Lives

I'll share an example of how spiritual amnesia appeared in my current incarnation. As a young adult I experienced frantic anxiety when my husband would leave the house without telling me goodbye. I knew it was an overreaction and assumed that it had to do with unresolved feelings of abandonment from my father leaving when I was five years old. While the level of angst I experienced didn't match up, it was the only reason I could fathom for the panic attacks.

Then, a few years ago, I accidentally listened to a past-life regression meditation. Up to that point I wasn't sure if I believed in past lives or not, but when it auto-played after another meditation I was listening to I just went with it. The host of the podcast guided me to visualize going into a tunnel that filled with fog, and at the end of the tunnel there was a door. When I opened and stepped through it I saw the year 1664. As the fog began to lift I found myself surrounded by tall golden wheat or hay, and I was in a foreign country.

Guided through the field I arrived at my home, a tiny shack where I saw my young daughter and son. Immediately my thoughts turned to my husband who was missing. He had left one day and never returned. Within the meditation I began crying, feeling deep emotional loss.

As the session progressed I was brought back through the tunnel to the present day. I opened my eyes and thought, "Wow, what a trip!" I wondered if what I just saw and experienced was true. I dried my eyes and rolled out of bed to start my day, but as my feet hit the ground my knees buckled. I fell to the floor, sobbing uncontrollably. I tried to get up but couldn't. After a few minutes I was able to gather myself together and press on with my day.

Many months later another regression meditation found its way to me, but this one was different because its intent was to *heal* past life pain. It took me through that same lifetime then guided me to change the story, so I visualized my husband staying with me and living a full life of love and peace as we grew old together.

When I came downstairs a few mornings later with my husband nowhere to be found, rather than feeling those familiar pangs of distress I felt an odd sense of peace and calm. So unexpected, the emotions puzzled me. I moved through my day and a couple of hours later it hit me. At last I understood that my lifelong anxiety had nothing to do with my dad leaving. It stemmed from a past-life trauma that carried over, impacting my behavior in this lifetime. The first regression brought it into my awareness, and the second one healed it. Since then my husband's unknown departures don't bother me in any way!

This example demonstrates how *you* always make perfect sense; you just usually don't have the insights and access to the reasoning.

Intuition

Until recently Western society placed more value on making informed, logical decisions based on data and critical thinking, but new research proves that letting your intuition weigh in—listening to what your gut tells you—renders better decisions. [22]

You've heard of intuition being an instinctual extrasensory perception. You recognize it when something doesn't *feel* right, or having a *knowing* about something but you just can't put your finger on how you know it.

HEAR THIS: The Wholly You

While you may consider them as two separate things, *the voice of intuition and your inner being are actually one and the same.* It makes sense that letting our intuition weigh in delivers better decisions. Of course it does! Tapping into and harnessing the wisdom across all your lifetimes as well as universal intelligence surely provides the best guidance.

Going one step further: Your incarnated self is only a portion of who you are. Your whole self—your whole soul—consists of 1) you in this carnation, and 2) your inner being.

HEAR THIS: Your Inner Being Is the *Bigger* Part of You

It's plausible Freud's iceberg theory relating to "the most important part of the mind lying below the surface"[23] is attributable to your inner being.

With this lens, it's possible to consider that the inner being part of your soul is having this life experience even *more* so than you, with your incarnated self representing the smaller part (as the visible tip of the iceberg), and the larger, submerged portion attributed to your inner being.

What a fascinating concept to consider!

CONNECTING DOTS: You're an 80% Match or Greater

Let's connect some dots here. First, recall from previous chapters these two things:

- All of your desires are in a holding room with a trap door in the floor held shut with a very old and worn piece of tape that's barely hanging on waiting for you to become a frequency match.
- Your thoughts must be in the vibrational frequency vicinity of your desired experience in order for the Universe's Search Engine to return a match.

With your inner being representing the greater part of your whole self, you are at all times minimally an 80% match to the frequency of your desires! Only 20% or less is needed to align frequencies to return your best life.

Disconnection with Your Inner Being

As the greater part of your soul, your inner being is always there, never taking its eyes off of you. While your inner being makes up the larger part of you and interconnectedness with your inner being is continuous and inseparable, what tends to happen as you're growing up is a squeezing off of that connectedness. This happens slowly over time, bit by bit as you take on other's programs as your own, sometimes to the point of being completely cut off. Imagine your connectedness when you're born like a brand new faucet, where the nozzle is clean and wide open. Water flows freely to and through it. Over time hard water calcification builds up, eventually blocking the flow until it's a meager stream.

As your disconnection increases, depression, disease, or a sense of loneliness and confusion increase because you're cutting yourself off from the primary part of who you are, holistically. Anyone separated from 80% of who they are is sure to have feelings of despair. It's not healthy and simply not how you were designed to live.

Re-connecting with Your Inner Being

Re-connecting requires that you tune into the voice of your inner being. Since connection to your inner being is your natural state, to re-connect all you have to do is switch from transmitter to receiver mode. As a human *being*, not a human *doing*, utilize the "just being" tools of mindfulness and meditation to tap in.

When you ask your inner being questions, responses come to you by way of words, images, or ideas popping into your head. A trivial example of how this works is when I was trying to eat healthier. I asked my inner being, "What should I have for lunch?" I heard loud and clear, "Soup." I didn't have any soup in the house, so I thought perhaps I misheard or made it up. Nevertheless, given my intention to actively listen to my inner being, I obediently went to my pantry looking for soup, but there was none. Moving towards the refrigerator I said, "Sorry, there isn't any soup." When I opened the refrigerator the first thing I saw was a bag of spinach staring at me. At that moment I realized I had been sautéing fresh spinach and tomatoes with butter earlier, and my daughter and I called it *spinach soup* because of the incredibly rich and delicious broth it yielded. I laughed and acknowledged, "Yes, soup! I get it now. Thank you!"

As you begin receiving guidance trust that your inner being knows and wants what is best for you, and will always lead you in the right direction. From personal experience opening the aperture and having a relationship with your inner being is quite liberating. I flash to the song "Jesus Take the Wheel" because that's what it feels like. I ask, "Where is it you want me to be?" and "What is the next step I should take?" Whatever I hear I follow with a sense of confidence.

Your inner being knows the path of least resistance to lead you where you need to be to achieve the goals set forth for this incarnation.

HEAR THIS: Your Inner Being Instigates Impulses, Thoughts, and Ideas

In Chapter 5 we learned that scientists theorize thoughts could potentially originate and reside in the cloud. What if that's partially true? What if thoughts are not triggered within the brain at all, and that's why scientist cannot locate their origin?

Your brain is a transmitter and receiver. This we know. What's new is, it is your inner being that produces origination of impulses, thoughts, and ideas within your brain.

While a significant concept to grasp, again it was Freud who termed the word unconscious, saying he "believed that much of what defines human behavior, including impulses, urges, thoughts, emotions and feelings, comes to the individual person in ways that she is not entirely cognizant of."[24] When connecting the dots between the scientific studies mentioned within this book alone, logic supports this theory.

Alignment with Your Inner Being

By becoming familiar with how you feel as new thoughts and ideas spring forth—seemingly from out of nowhere—you'll realize how this works. It's why inspiration feels so good. That boosted energy and those positive feelings come from harmony with your inner being.

Often, when ideas are downloaded to me my energy surges into such high vibes that I have a hard time falling asleep. You've probably experienced the same thing when a great idea hit you. That high-flying sense of elation comes from pure alignment between you and your inner being. Your excitement multiplies with your inner being's excitement, resulting in your energy being off the charts!

HEAR THIS: Feelings Are Your Sixth Sense

As your guide, feelings *always* tell you where you are in relation to alignment with your inner being. When you're feeling good there is alignment. When you're not, there's misalignment. This rule is a constant, and it's why feelings are indeed your sixth sense.

You Have Complete Control

While initial thoughts, ideas, and impulses are triggered by your inner being, what you choose to contemplate comes from you in this carnation as the thinker of your thoughts. What you do with what's downloaded to you is completely your prerogative. It's your choice to ignore or heed those ideas and inspirations.

Guides

Besides inner being connectedness, in the realm of metaphysics many point to the existence of spirit guides that are assigned to you throughout your lifetime to watch over and protect you, often having an area of expertise dialed in to the help you need. In most cases you have more than one guide and they can be with you for this lifetime, decades, or a few years. The period of time depends on how long they're providing value.

As you progress and evolve your thinking, higher frequency guides step in to assist you on your continued path of expansion and discovery, helping you achieve upper levels of vibrational frequency. Like your inner being, assigned guides are also with you at all times, never taking their eyes off of you.

Synchronicity

If you look for it, you will begin noticing your inner being and guide's hands in your life by way of synchronicity. You've always seen the help, but you've called them crazy coincidences. In fact, coincidences are just coinciding incidents.

For instance, one day I asked for guidance during a meditation. I was feeling frustrated and unsure about my writing so I asked, "Should I write this book?" There was no immediate response. Five minutes later I jumped into my car and "magically" the host of the podcast I tuned into said, "It's like being called to write a book. Even if someone told you to stop, you couldn't stop yourself. You have to write the book. You must. It's your calling." Okay got it, and thank you!

Superpowers Are Your Birthright

Connecting to your inner being provides insights that propel you onto your path quicker, so use your inborn connection to establish and foster that relationship. Combining the power of thoughts to control what the Universe's Search Engine returns, coupled with the power of the metaphysical, gives you superpowers, in the plural! Both work together in a concerted effort to bring forth what you desire. When leveraged to the fullest there's nothing that can stop you from receiving and achieving all you wish for.

Key Principles

1. Metaphysics is the concern or interest in things other than the material and physical.
2. Almost everyone believes in something greater than themselves.
3. You are a soul manifesting in physical form.
4. Your soul has all experiences, knowledge, and wisdom from all lifetimes and is a powerful source of intelligence.
5. Interconnectedness is being connected to all things in the Universe.
6. Intuition is an automatic sense that provides guidance and better decision-making.

7. Your inner being is also known as your intuition.
8. Your whole soul consists of your incarnated self and your inner being.
9. Your inner being is the larger part of who you are.
10. Your inner being is connected to Source.
11. Connection to your inner being is your natural state of being.
12. Foster a relationship with your intuition by asking, "What can I do for you today?"
13. Initial thoughts, ideas and memories are initiated by your inner being.
14. Guides are assigned to you throughout your lifetime watching over and providing guidance.
15. Connection to spirit energies is your birthright and a superpower.

CHAPTER 9
BODY MATTERS

*"You are the Universe manifesting through a human
nervous system and becoming self-aware."*
—Deepak Chopra

While the energies at play creating and impacting your life are completely invisible, you live in a material world with a physical body. So we turn our attention to the soul-body connection to further challenge perspectives, increase self-alignment and bring about greater peace, self-care and compassion.

Your Amazing Body

Your heart began pumping blood throughout your body before you were born, and that has continued every second of the day without any thought or interference from you. Your lungs take in and circulate oxygen to each of your trillion cells twenty-four seven. If you are fortunate enough to have them, your legs walked you into kindergarten and your last job interview. Your body has aided you in showing affection to loved ones by way of hugs and kisses, and enabled your glee to shine through with that smile captured in your favorite photo, and so on.

Your body—a carbon-based high-tech machine—facilitates your movement and interaction in this world, including the enjoyment of earthly experiences like smelling cookies baking, scaling mountains, conceiving and bearing children, and doing the laundry too!

Enlightenment: I love My Body!

Living life as a soul and not as a body changes everything. Awareness that you are not your external presence, but rather pure energy inhabiting a physical body, is the secret to enlightenment. With this perspective you're empowered to engage all facets of the whole you to see things clearer, more as they truly are.

When you recognize that your body is not who you are it gives you the ability to step away from self-judgment and move into self-loving. You are set free to love your body—your arms, your feet, nose, ears, stomach and digestive system—because, wow, what an amazing job they do for you! Every trip to the bathroom is a marvel and an opportunity to appreciate the miracle of your body. It works very hard on your behalf, taking the food you consume, processing it, straining out nutrients to fuel your body and at the same time removing what it cannot use, turning it into waste and moving it out.

How many years have you had the privilege of a working colon? Have you ever been grateful for it—or better yet *to* it?

Your Cherished Partner

Your body is your cherished partner and you are responsible for its care and wellbeing. Similar to how you care for a mate, child, or beloved pet, foster a relationship with your body. Honor the soul-body bond with respect, love, kindness, and gratitude. As you do you'll find yourself taking better care of your body by choosing healthier foods, not over feeding it, and giving it enough rest.

This relationship is a mutually beneficial partnership because the better care you take of your body, the better you feel and the more energy and vitality you have.

Body Intelligence

I would guess that you've never asked your body something, but I encourage you to try it. When you wake up in the morning ask your body, "What do you need from me today?" or "What can I do for you that'll make you feel special?"

Before going to sleep each night thank your body for the fantastic job it did, and check in by performing a body scan. If you haven't done a body scan before, start by closing your eyes and taking a few deep breaths before bringing your attention to each toe, then your feet, then ankles, continuing upwards until you've reached the top of your head. Locate any tension or aching and introduce extra loving oxygen by breathing in and visualizing that air being moved into that area, and feel the release.

Offer Kindness and Compassion

Viewing your body as your beloved partner should change your tone when your body becomes sick, gets injured, or those times when you just "don't feel good" for no apparent reason. Transition from a state of harsh judgment, frustration, and disappointment by shifting from asking "What's wrong with *me*?" to "I'm sorry *you're* not feeling well. What can I do to take care of *you*?"

Besides switching pronouns from "me" to "you," can you feel the energy pivot from negative to positive? Being angry or disappointed in your body isn't helpful or healthy. Offering loving kindness, compassion, care, and tenderness as you would for a sick loved one is helpful and enables quicker healing—and appreciation from your body!

HEAR THIS: The Exquisiteness of Feeling

In the Bible Book of Genesis there's a story about angels that looked down on Earth and became envious of men able to experience pleasures of the flesh. These angels wanted to feel these sensations, so against God's order they took the form of man, married, and had children. Their offspring were giants called Nephilim, superhuman in strength and size. Big bullies, these fallen angels and Nephilim's were all killed off in the flood of Noah.[25]

The point of this story is: Angels chose to leave heaven and disobey a direct command from God for the opportunity to experience tactile feelings. This tells us that the ability to feel is a great and enviable gift! The human shell provides your soul with opportunities to experience smelling the roses, feeling the grass between your toes, warm water trickling down your body in the shower, wind and sunlight caressing your face, savoring the taste of chocolate and the way it melts in your mouth, and so on, and so on, and so on.

This Is Your Turn

Become conscious of everything your body experiences by way of feelings, from what it's like to be out of breath, the satisfying feeling of a great stretch, walking hand in hand with your child, gazing into your loved one's eyes, giggling so hard your stomach and cheeks hurt, and giving a hefty hug to comfort someone.

You are having a turn on this planet as a physical being. When you are not living in the moment, you lose the beauty of your turn. You bypass and cheat yourself out of the full experience. Touching, feeling, talking, smelling, and breathing will be unavailable to you when you leave this earth plane, so while you have your physical body enjoy and appreciate the magnificence of it!

Mind-Body Connection

The mind-body connection has to do with how your thoughts have a direct correlation to the health of your body on a molecular level, where your cells react to everything you think and say. More than thirty years ago Louise Hay wrote a book about the mind-body connection entitled *You Can Heal Your Life.* While considered a maverick in her time, over the past three to four decades there have been numerous scientific studies validating her work.

Heart-Mind Connection

You may have been taught that research and facts were king, and to be objective and steer clear of feelings that muddied the waters. And, maybe you were also taught that the brain was the central processing unit controlling *everything,* with the heart relegated to emotions and feelings. Recent studies have proved otherwise, showing that your heart is also an intelligent organ with its own network of neurons and neurotransmitters that have the capacity to trigger thoughts and send messages that affect the brain's activity.[26] Isn't that amazing?

With scientific proof of the heart-mind connection it's important to let *both* weigh in to make better decisions. Do this by asking your heart, "How do you feel about that?" or "What would that feel like?" and let the answers inform your decisions.

Ego Vs. Your Body

About ten years ago I was listening to a lot of self-improvement CDs that ego-shamed, espousing how bad the ego was. I interpreted the ego as the voice telling you *anything* positive about yourself.

My tendency to take things too literally, coupled with a strong desire for improvement and growth, made me quick to become self-aware of any kind words of praise or accolades. When I thought to myself, "You did a great job during that presentation," immediately I pointed a finger to my ego and said, "Ah-ha, there you are. That's you giving me too much credit." If I had the thought, "You look good today!" I'd jump right back to say, "Boy, I see you ego and you're not going to get away with that." Again and again, I caught all self-praise and congratulations from large to minute and stifled them to death. Over a period of a couple of years, my self-esteem suffered tragically, shriveling up all my self-confidence. It was not a healthy, enjoyable place to be.

The next time you knock that presentation out of the park, give yourself the kudos you deserve. It's okay and even healthy to acknowledge your strengths. It's also fine to say, "I look hot today." Complimenting and acknowledging your body and successes does not a narcissist make! Trust that if you were going to be a narcissist, you'd already be one.

To tell the difference between what your ego is saying versus what your body, inner being, or guides are saying, look for a selfish, self-serving direction having something to do with you getting ahead or doing better to the detriment of others. However, whatever you do, don't confuse self-serving with *self-caring*. Nurturing your body and soul is healthy and good, even necessary.

HEAR THIS: The Diamond Rule Is to Love You

Undoubtedly you've heard the golden rule that states, "Love thy neighbor as you love thyself."[27] I grew up with at least eight hours of bible study per week, so I know this scripture well. What's interesting is that across any religion the emphasis always falls on loving others. But if you look again, quite clearly this scripture implies that your natural state of being is that you *love thyself.* In fact, in order to love others you must first love yourself and if you are unable to do so, then you don't have the capacity to truly love others.

If the golden rule is to treat others the way you want to be treated, and the platinum rule is to treat others the way *they* want to be treated, then the *diamond rule* is to love you! Love your whole self, inclusive of your amazing body.

Self-Talk

Does any of this negative self-talk sound familiar? "I'm so fat!" "I hate my legs!" "I'm so ugly!" Now think about the Universe's Search Engine positioned at the ready to pick up and process every thought. Self-loathing thoughts bundled with disgust or shame produce terribly low vibes. These bundled thoughts are sure to return some negative juju, not to mention poisoning your cells.

Since it takes at least five positive statements to erase a single negative one,[28] keep and eye out for negative self-talk directed to your body, and for that matter to your character, intelligence, or temperament as it is equally harmful. With your growing awareness, shift to the high frequency vibration of appreciation, or better yet the highest frequency you can emit: Love.

Ending all forms of toxic self-talk is possible and has the power to heal you.

Affirmations, Take Two

If you have negative body image programming, here are some positive body affirmations you can use to rock the needle out of the groove:

- MY BODY LOVES ME
- FOOD IS MY FRIEND
- MY BODY ENJOYS EXERCISING
- MY BODY DESERVES LOVE
- MY BODY IS A GIFT
- I AM BLESSED TO BE AGING
- MY BODY IS NOT ME
- BEING FAT IS NOT MY IDENTITY
- BEING SKINNY IS NOT MY IDENTITY
- I CAN BE HEALTHY AT ANY SIZE

Key Principles

1. Your soul lives in a material world in a human form with a strong interconnectedness between the soul and body.

2. Your body is a tool facilitating your ability to live life on this planet.

3. Awareness that you are not your external presence but rather pure energy inhabiting a physical body is the secret to enlightenment.

4. Move from self-judgment into self-loving.

5. Your body is intelligent. Check in and offer gratitude for the work it performs and the experiences it affords you.

6. View your body as your cherished partner, offering kindness and compassion.

7. Don't take your human senses for granted, as they are not carried into spirit form.

8. Your thoughts also emanate throughout your body.

9. There's a heart-mind connection so it's important to listen to your heart to render better decisions.

10. Giving your body and yourself credit and gratitude does not a narcissist make!

11. The golden rule is to love others, the diamond rule is to love you.

CHAPTER 10
PURPOSE MATTERS

*"If you can't figure out your purpose, figure out your passion.
For your passion will lead you right into your purpose."*
—Bishop T.D. Jakes

When you're not living in your purpose you feel a gnawing sense of dissatisfaction, which stems from misalignment with your inner being. This chapter explores how to (re)discover your purpose through practical guidance and techniques to move you into alignment and restore happiness.

Live Life in Joy

First and foremost, the things that you're passionate about are not random. They are your calling. Being absorbed in your passion brings you joy, and when you're in joy you are living your purpose. That's it. No riddle me this or riddle me that. If you're not living in joy then you are off your mark. It really is that straightforward because feelings of joy indicate resonance with your inner being and that alignment is everything!

Second and equally significant, you don't have to achieve anything to be worthy of being here. There is nothing you need to do to prove your worth. By virtue of you being alive, you are worthy and perfectly perfect.

If this doesn't resonate, the next time you see a flower I want you to stop and get up real nice and close so you're able to take a good look at the blossom itself. Notice the poise of the flower doing exactly what it was meant to do. It sprouted, budded, and blossomed not into a tree, not into a cactus, but into the species of flower as defined by its DNA. So too were you born with a specific temperament, personality type, strengths and weaknesses, and together you could not be any more perfect at being you. In all of your glorious uniqueness, you're like no one else (truly another superpower). What an extraordinarily beautiful species you are!

Third, it isn't by accident that you're on this planet. If you're here, room was made for you to be here in this place and time, and you had a reason for coming.

Life Plan

Before incarnating into this lifetime you set forth a life plan with goals for how you wanted to show up, what you wanted to learn, how you wanted to expand or evolve the planet. While spiritual amnesia blocks your memory of those intentions, your inner being hasn't forgotten and is always at work guiding you in that direction *by what feels good.*

When you are fulfilling your life plan your heart is filled with joy and there's a sense of contentment, which is completely related to your knowing that this is exactly where you're supposed to be. Here's what that looks like. If my purpose is to be a teacher, then being a teacher makes me happy and fulfilled. But if my purpose is to be a teacher and I'm selling cars, it's likely I will be dissatisfied. Eventually, I may become depressed, and I'll have a nagging sense that I'm not where I should be.

Let Your Feelings Be Your Guide

Generally speaking, and barring chemical or hormonal imbalances, being unhappy and feeling unworthy as a perpetual state of being is a sign of misalignment with your inner being. Being out of harmony will always cause you discomfort and dissatisfaction, and that's intentional.

Remembering that emotions are your GPS, feeling depressed, unhappy, or unworthy are cues alerting you to what you're thinking about, and trying to wake you up to the fact that change is needed. When you don't take heed and make shifts, that disharmony has the potential to make you sick, given your state of dis-ease.

Here's a scenario about how feelings show up to let you know you're not in alignment with your inner being and purpose. Let's say you've turned into an epic couch potato. The first day or two of doing nothing but gorging on soda and potato chips, binge watching *Breaking Bad* and not showering were glorious. You probably needed the rest! After another couple of days though, the couch potato-kingdom satisfaction wanes. Instead of feeling refreshed and reenergized, you feel tired and sluggish. Your self-confidence and drive are diminishing and you're slipping into a depression, suffering from guilt over all of the things you know you could be doing, but aren't. All of those *feelings* are intended to instigate change by letting you know loud and clear, "Nope, being a couch potato is not your purpose!"

Happiness Barometer

Hospital patients use a scale to quantify their level of pain. Let's use a similar scale to measure how close or how far you are from living in your purpose. Where do you fall on the happiness barometer?

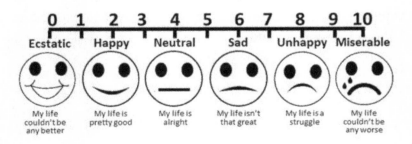

Everyone's goal is between zero and two. If you rate yourself in this range it's likely you're doing what fulfills you and aligns to what matters to you most. If you fall between three and six it's possible that you're going through the motions, doing what's expected of you and what's necessary like holding down a job to ensure your family is taken care of, but it doesn't do much to fulfill or bring you joy.

If you're between seven and ten your level of dissatisfaction is prompting life changes. Look at this challenging time as the Universe readying you for transformation. When you're in this difficult space pay attention and grab the lessons, while looking for and expecting the silver lining (see Chapter 11).

Happiness as Your Natural State of Being

I have heard it said that no one deserves to be happy, and that believing so is a false sense of entitlement. I disagree. I believe whole-heartedly that you have a fundamental right to happiness, and what's more it's your responsibility! When you perceive your life to be a gift or like your choice to take a turn here, then it's incumbent upon you to value and utilize it by spending your time doing things that bring you the most joy to the best of your ability.

(Re)Discovering Your Purpose

Your passions never fail to lead you to your purpose. To remember your purpose, define what matters to you most (passions), and what makes you the happiest (joy). Then identify what made you stand out from everybody else when you were a kid. What made you different?

While it may have been considered by some as a negative or a fault, typically that uniqueness turns out to be your greatest gift(s). For instance, as an inquisitive child I asked lots of questions—I mean a lot of questions—to the point my family would say to me, "You're so irritating!" Being inquisitive I sought to understand, asking, "Why am I so irritating?" To which they responded, "That's why!"

On top of that I'm inclined to take things much more literally than others. Both atypical behaviors turned out to be my greatest strengths, contributing to my successful career across Silicon Valley companies with an ability to dissect, understand, and build out processes at both granular and visionary levels better than most.

Next, reflect back on what you used to do for fun and what came natural to you when you were young. What were your inborn strengths? Often times your natural talents were taken for granted because they came so easily to you that you wrongly assumed it must be effortless for everyone else too.

Those answers provide the breadcrumbs that lead you back to your inner being and onto the path of living your life on-purpose, doing what you're meant to be doing.

Use the Force

If you have trouble narrowing in on your gifts and passions, connect to your inner being, Source, and guides through meditation and mindfulness. Turn down transmitter-mode and become the receiver to obtain clarity. Your source-force is always there, standing by at the ready to help.

You Matter

You, like everyone, matter. You deserve to be happy and that's totally possible if you take control as the deliberate creator of your life experiences, stepping into the shoes that you came to fill. Be unapologetic in claiming what you desire, and lean into trusting that there's a reason for it.

Your ideal state is different from the next person because you and your purpose are different. Knowing what you want and going for it is not selfish, it is being authentic to who you are and who you're meant to be. There is plenty of room for everyone to live their best life in the fulfillment of their dreams.

Follow Your Bliss

Everything in life is fluid, constantly moving and changing. This applies to your purpose as well. As you achieve one purpose another follows. You can serve numerous purposes, sometimes in the same vein and sometimes in a different one altogether.

Pay attention to your feelings as they will let you know when your purpose has changed. Let them guide you to continual expansion and joy. Be open and flexible. As they say, follow your bliss.

Getting Stuck

From personal experience, being stuck feels like you've lived long enough and if the ride were over you'd be okay with it. You feel burnt out, lost, miserable, anxious, or depressed. Those feelings are signals trying to wake you up to the fact that you are not living in your purpose.

Taking care of yourself and a family, ensuring they have food and a roof over their heads is a high priority. I get it. So when you are in a dead-end job that no longer aligns with your joy you may feel trapped and believe there's no way to break free. As a result, year after year you go through the motions until there's little of your precious energy left.

Bring the Joy!

While it appears you aren't free to make life or career changes due to your circumstances, you always have the opportunity to find purpose alignment (joy) in your current situation. For instance, if you love to cook and always wanted to be a chef but your job is a Compliance Officer, bring colleagues dishes or organize a cross-department chili cook-off. Take cooking classes or volunteer to barbeque at company picnics or cook at a shelter. Look for ways to feed (align with) your inner being to deliver a sense of fulfillment and joy.

During my time at a local junior college my English teacher told our class the story of Sisyphus, who was cursed to carry an immense boulder up a hill only to watch it roll back down for eternity. Mr. Tiernan colored the story with details of the blazing heat, bitter cold, and tedious monotony before asking, "How do you think Sisyphus felt about this burden?" The answer was, in order to perform this menial task day in and day out Sisyphus had to love it! He grew an appreciation for all the gifts this job gave him by way of chiseling and sculpting his muscles, affording him peace and quiet, time to think, and so on.

It's Your Choice

Just as Sisyphus sought out, found, and focused on the gifts the power to switch the lens of negativity to a lens of gratitude is possible because there's always something to be grateful for. You just have to decide to bring the joy. It's a decision. In all cases you get to *choose* what to focus on and the energy that you bring.

Life Phases

As a caveat to making it a priority to live in joy, it's important to note that there are phases of life that can make this challenging. It could be adjustment periods like an illness, or suffering a loss. In these episodes you can expect the ground underneath you to shift making it impossible to focus on fully living in joy as you expend all your energy working to acclimate to your new life. In these cases it's normal for your joy to dim.

Exercise loving kindness and compassion for yourself, and leverage the coping skills in the next chapter to assist you in moving through life's difficult times.

Key Principles

1. Disharmony with your inner being is felt as unhappiness and a dis-ease that can manifest as a disease or illness.
2. Your purpose is to live in joy.
3. There is nothing you need to do to prove your worth.
4. It isn't by accident that you're here and room was made just for you.
5. Feelings are blessings intended to instigate change.
6. Happiness is your natural state of being. You deserve to be happy.
7. Following the breadcrumbs of what brings you joy will always lead you to your purpose.
8. Your purpose is fluid. As you achieve one another follows. Remain open and flexible in following your bliss.
9. Get unstuck by bringing the joy.
10. Offer loving compassion to yourself through life phases that make living in joy challenging.

CHAPTER 11
COPING MATTERS

"As you say goodbye to lingering disappointments and unattended grief, you will discover that every person, situation and painful incident comes bearing gifts."
—Debbie Ford

Life continues to come your way. Part of living on this earth plane is the reality that there is contrast, which can bring pain, hardship, and grief. This chapter provides coping skills intended to ease your suffering, expedite healing, and expand your perspective so you spend minimum energy sending negative commands to the Universe's Search Engine.

Let's first address the elephant in the room before moving any further. More than half of this book carefully and succinctly explained precisely how your thoughts are responsible for returning your reality. Recall Dr. Wayne Dyer's quote, "No matter how much you protest you are totally responsible for everything that happens to you in your life." When you encounter painful experiences it's important to be 100% honest with yourself to reveal thoughts that brought the incident to fruition.

However, there are other factors that come into play that are outside your span of control. In addition to metaphysical forces, what other people are thinking or doing that brings forth their reality could impact you.

Regardless of how a situation came to be, leverage the coping skills in this chapter that resonate with you to ju-jitsu your energy and ease your heartache.

Life's Stretch Assignments

In Corporate America the term "stretch assignment" is code for projects assigned to employees outside of their day-to-day job that are designed to give those desiring career advancement an opportunity to learn, grow, and prove themselves. When you're given a stretch assignment it conveys management's confidence in you. If the project is completed successfully you've demonstrated your ability to take on more responsibility, so likely you're next in line for a promotion.

When a life experience presents pain or discomfort, there's an opportunity to view the challenge as a stretch assignment, where there will be learning and growth. In Ainslie MacLeod's book, *The Instruction: Living the Life You Intended,* he guides readers enduring hardships to perform investigations to search for lessons and opportunities saying, "What an investigation does is to turn even the most unpleasant experience into an opportunity for growth."[29]

When you're given a stretch assignment in the form of a painful or challenging life experience, it may be possible to view it through the lens of a vote of confidence that you're ready for expansion.

Change Is Constant

It's universal law that everything is in a constant state of motion and that motion produces constant change. For the vast majority of people, however, change is difficult—even when it's considered positive. Shifts, growth, expansion—whether perceived as good or bad—come from change, and all come to teach and guide you, which is what this earth plane is for. It's the only plane where you're able to practice, learn, and expand.

Grief Is Real

When you experience the loss of a loved one, the end of a relationship, a health crisis, losing a job or your home it's important to allow yourself to grieve. Grief is exceedingly painful and should be respected, acknowledged, and honored. Not many escape experiencing grief or the accompanying isolation of knowing that no one can help you because there's nothing anyone can do to change what has happened.

When my oldest son was in the hospital fighting for his life, I found knowing the seven stages of grief (shock, denial, guilt, anger, bargaining, depression, and hope) extremely helpful, both as a way to chart my progress through the pain and as validation that my feelings were normal, expected, and healthy. Thankfully, he made a full recovery and today he's living a beautiful life.

The Importance of Mourning

Everyone mourns differently. There's no right or wrong way to grieve. Generally, you'll go back and forth between the stages in random order. There's no defined timeline for how long the process takes. The key is to not avoid grief. Doing so renders you stuck, increasing the amount of your suffering by elongating the healing process. You also introduce more pain when you bury your head in the sand by using drugs, alcohol or becoming a workaholic. These negative vices destroy your body and your relationships, which in the end certainly causes more suffering.

If you're just trying to survive, then you aren't allowing yourself the space to mourn either. Holding on to old energy doesn't allow for the healing, so while excruciating, the easiest way out is through. Allow yourself to be human and practice much self-love and compassion. Every morning ask, "What can I do to be kind to myself today?" Then do it!

Look at the incident that brought this grief as a stretch assignment that will change you forever in some very positive and profound ways. Cling to the fact that everything in life is fluid, and this too shall pass. While it may not feel like it, no storm lasts forever. Your job is to absorb the experience by being grateful for what was, and take away the lessons and as much personal growth as possible.

What If?

When we are faced with painful or challenging life experiences, the power of "what if" can work its magic to shift our thinking:

- *What if* 1960s radical activist Bill Ayers's quote, "To be a human being is to suffer," is a belief system that delivers an expectation that you will suffer?
- When someone dies I have heard it said, "It must've been their time." What if that's true and it was their time? *What if* their death-date was predetermined when they entered the world and, while it was a surprise to you, it wasn't a surprise to their inner being or Source?
- *What if* when a baby dies it was a soul who chose to come into the world for a brief period of time to teach the parents about love, loss and empathy?
- *What if* those incarnating with disabilities or differing sexual or gender preferences are the most courageous of us all, intentionally choosing to challenge perspectives, inspire unconditional love and evolve the planet?

Other pivoting questions are:

- *What if* you looked at a painful or challenging life experience as if it were *your choice*? What would that look like?
- *What if* instead of asking, "Why is this happening *to* me," you ask "Why is this happening *for* me?"

The following example highlights beautifully the benefits of posing this last "what if" question. A few years ago, a routine medical test came back with abnormal results. I asked my doctor if I could simply retake the test because I felt fine and had no other symptoms. She rejected this request and insisted on a colonoscopy, which requires careful preparation to completely empty the colon. Days prior to the procedure, I stopped consuming vitamins, food, coffee, and milk. This meant I was off of my beloved Nespresso with steamed hearty whole milk for three solid days!

The test went routinely, with no issues discovered. However, after the procedure I noticed I was feeling better than usual. Over the past couple of years my body stiffness and aching had become progressively worse to the point of losing the ability to turn my neck. Yet post-procedure I freely rotated my head with absolutely no restriction or pain, and my body no longer hurt.

Dancing around, swiveling my head to and fro, and marching with high knee lifts I paraded in front of my husband exclaiming, "Look at me! Look at me! I can move and nothing hurts!"

With this complete disappearance of pain I realized the root cause of my condition must be something I was ingesting. Carefully I reintroduced items one by one back into my diet. On the day I added milk my neck began to stiffen and ache, and that night I wrestled to find a comfortable spot on my pillow. Turns out, milk is an inflammatory for me. Since this discovery I've eliminated milk from my diet and have been free from constant pain, which has substantially improved my quality of life.

While this may seem like a trivial example, it's an effective one that illustrates how something happened "for" me rather than "to" me. Of course, I wasn't pleased when my test results showed an abnormality, and surely I didn't want a colonoscopy, but the end result—the discovery of the source of my chronic pain—was certainly a gift!

There's a Master Plan

There's a well-known biblical story of Job who had a loving wife, ten children, and massive riches. He was known across the land as God-loving, God-fearing, and God-serving, but inexplicably Job lost everything in one fell swoop. Coupled with his deep emotional grief, he was afflicted with skin lesions causing great physical pain. Job's friends said he must've done something wrong to deserve such agony. Adding insult to injury, they also told him his children brought their deaths upon themselves. Job wished to die, lamenting at the injustice, but at the same time he acknowledged God's unlimited power and his own inability to know the master plan, and so he kept his faith.

What Job didn't know was that he was at the center of a dispute between God and Satan, where Satan argued that Job only loved and worshiped Him because He blessed him with wealth. God gave Satan permission to torment Job short of taking his life to prove that Job's love wasn't contingent on his abundance. The story ends with God blessing Job with an exceptionally long life to enjoy his new wife, more children and twice as many riches.[30]

The applicable concept here is that there is a master plan that is *unknowable* to you, always. It's something beyond your mind. For instance, if you lose your job it's impossible to see the better job around the corner. It's easy to become angry when you need to move back home, not seeing the beautiful gift affording you the honor of taking care of your mother who is diagnosed with terminal cancer soon afterwards. Or, when a relationship ends it's difficult to see that you're making room for your soulmate who is working their way to you.

Divine Perfection

Divine perfection is the concept that there are no mistakes, and that at every moment of every day everything is as it should be. The grand master plan and divine plan includes your life plan. It is divinely orchestrated and unfolding exactly as it should. Having faith in this allows you to rest assured that you're exactly where you're supposed to be.

Free Will

While there's a master and divine plan, you are not a robot because you exercise free will. Freud believed "there is a smaller region from which we can actively receive and analyze information in our conscious, waking mind. This small part is what actually controls the traits and behaviors typically labeled personality."[31]

Because you are always the thinker of your thoughts, it's completely your discretion what you do with inspirations and ideas instigated from your inner being, whether you heed them or disregard them. With a myriad of things to ponder, it's completely your choice what to spend time thinking about. So when it's said that "everything that happens has been orchestrated to happen and is on-purpose" and "you're exactly where you are supposed to be" your creationist power falls into that mix.

HEAR THIS: Angels Exercise Free Will

As an interesting and related side note, even angels exercise free will as demonstrated in the Genesis story of the angels that looked down on Earth and became envious of men who were able to experience the pleasures of the flesh. Those angels disobeyed a direct command from God, coming to Earth to take the form of man, marry, and have children.[32]

Exercise Non-Judgment

Because you can't know the inner workings of the master plan, when something hasn't turned out the way you hoped it would it's wise to lean into non-judgment rather than judging the hows and whys (demonstrating non-acceptance). The following parable of the Chinese Farmer models perfectly executed non-judgment:

Once there was a Chinese farmer who worked his poor farm together with his son and their horse. When the horse ran off one day, neighbors came to say, "How unfortunate for you!" The farmer replied, "Maybe yes, maybe no."

When the horse returned, followed by a herd of wild horses, the neighbors gathered around and exclaimed, "What good luck for you!" The farmer stayed calm and replied, "Maybe yes, maybe no."

While trying to tame one of wild horses, the farmer's son fell and broke his leg. He had to rest up and couldn't help with the farm chores. "How sad for you," the neighbors cried. "Maybe yes, maybe no," said the farmer.

Shortly thereafter, a neighboring army threatened the farmer's village. All the young men in the village were drafted to fight the invaders. Many died. But the farmer's son had been left out of the fighting because of his broken leg. People said to the farmer, "What a good thing your son couldn't fight!" "Maybe yes, maybe no," was all the farmer said. [33]

Choose the Path of Least Resistance

When you find yourself in friction of any kind, leverage the law of least resistance by moving into the space of allowing. Imagine giving up, giving in, letting go, and surrendering. This exercise releases resistance, relieves pressure and delivers a sense of peace and calm.

Guided meditations are very helpful in moving you into this frame of mind as well, shifting perspectives and easing your pain.

You Always Have a Choice

Thinking you have no choice is a belief system. Knowing belief systems are blocks of thoughts that have become stuck, you can dissolve them by pivoting from "There's nothing I can do" to asking "What can I do?" and "What if" questions.

When you lose a loved one it's true that you were not given a choice. The focus here is how you *choose* to handle the loss. What will you spend your time thinking about and focusing on?

Contrast Expands You

Another way to change your perspective is to look at difficult life experiences as a gift of contrast, providing you with a much better understanding of yourself. Contrast provides clarity on what you like and want, and what you don't like and don't want. For instance, do you know what it's like to be flat broke and unable to pay your bills? If so, that contrast makes you ever so grateful when you have plenty of money. Contrast sharpens preferences across all facets of your life, including wealth, health, and love.

Focus on What You Want, Not the Absence of It

What you want and the absence of it are opposite sides of the same coin. To illustrate the importance of this positioning, consider how we think about relationships:

- o I *hate* it when my husband/wife/child/boss treats me this way.
  - Focuses on what you don't want.
  - Sends negative vibes.
  - Returns more of what you do not want.

- o I *love* it when my husband/wife/child/boss treats me this way.
  - Focuses on what you do want.
  - Sends positive vibes.
  - Returns more of what you do want.

Remember, the frequencies between what you want and the absence of it are *opposite in polarity* and therefore attract very different life experiences. If you find it difficult to stop thinking about what you don't want, try focusing on the solution rather than the problem, and if that's too difficult switch tracks altogether and think about a totally unrelated topic.

Opportunity for Others to Expand and Practice Compassion

Difficult experiences provide opportunities for others to expand, question their belief systems, and adjust their perspectives as well. Here's how that works: When someone sees you suffering over the loss of your job, what do they do? They reflect on their job—the very job they were complaining about yesterday—and shift into gratitude.

Observing someone else making poor decisions works in the same way. Not only do they learn the lesson, but others learn as well. Once I heard Oprah say, "I love to learn from others. I see what they're going through and learn the lesson so I don't have to go through it myself."

In addition, everyone likes to feel valued, contribute, and make a difference. When someone is suffering it provides others with an opportunity to help and practice love and compassion.

Use Appreciation to Pivot into Acceptance

Appreciation is an inclusive energy so when you're in the space of it there is unconditional acceptance. Also, since you can only have one thought at a time, when you're appreciating something your thoughts simply cannot be on something else so it provides a break from what's bothering you.

Appreciation also resonates to inspire and promote health and well-being. When you find it difficult to move away from negative thoughts and feelings, move into appreciation by taking a walk, starting an appreciation journal, or making a list of three things you're grateful for each and every day.

COMPLETE EXERCISE 8: FOCUS SHIFTER

- Description: Shift your focus to shorten the duration of suffering.
- Time allocation: 25 minutes
- Page 164
- Online: <u>anitamscott.com/ex8</u> — Password (case sensitive): focus

---

Find the Gift

My first book, *Greater than Grateful*, captures some of my personal challenges. During the tough times I always found something to be grateful for. There really is a gift in all situations no matter how difficult. Rather than focusing on the pain of the situation, choose to look for and expect the unexpected gifts, and they will be there. Search for the silver lining, noting that the gift may be in the lesson and expansion.

In an interview with David Laroche, entitled "Activate Your Potential," Michael Beckwith said, "You discover your happiness when you're able to see that in every circumstance there is possibility, there's potential, and there's an energy behind it pushing you to a greater expression of who and what you really are."[34]

I Deserve to Suffer

As you begin feeling better, pay attention if your mind tells you a story that feeling good is not okay. The same goes for thinking you have the right to feel bad, so while you were coming up for air you *choose* to turn back and marinate in your heartache.

Everyone grieves differently, and of course you certainly have a right to feel bad, but if levity and moments of joy work their way to you to break up the monotony of pain, grab ahold of them because you have a fundamental right to be happy. Never suffer for suffering sake.

ADDITIONAL COPING SKILLS

Sometimes you just have a bad day. When the previous coping skills are overkill for the situation at hand, use some of the following techniques to shift your focus and increase the quality of your thoughts.

Faux Smiling

It's been scientifically proven that when you smile—even when it's not sincere—it sends messages throughout your body and brain that actually makes you feel better.[35]

Thanks to entrainment, another benefit of smiling is that it causes others to smile back, which in turn tends to make you feel better as those positive vibes are received by you.

Do for Others

Consider giving yourself the gift of space away from your problems by helping someone else in need. Helping others takes the focus off you, providing relief and the chance to recharge so you're able to refocus with a greater sense of clarity. Creating space presents the opportunity to pivot thoughts from negative to positive increasing thought quality and frequency, and therefore what the Universe's Search Engine returns.

Let the Music Move You

Music is pure vibration so turning on the radio and listening to your favorite upbeat songs does wonders in improving energy by lifting your vibratory frequency. Stand up, sing, and dance around even if you don't feel like it. Make a conscious effort to shake up your energy and change your focus. Literally and figuratively, your thoughts will move to the music and before you know it you'll be emitting higher vibes and feeling much better.

Movies

Going to the movies is a tried and true way to escape from what's going on in your life. Similar to helping others or dancing to upbeat music, movies provide space between you and the issue, allowing room for recharging and clarity.

Don't forget about those mirror neurons acting like a funnel at the top of your head. Select positive, funny, joyful movies that won't transmit any negative thoughts on your behalf.

Tomorrow Is a New Day

When all else fails it's helpful to know that every new day brings the prospect of starting fresh and making different choices. Throughout all of your life's challenges do your utmost to practice self-love, kindness, and compassion.

Key Principles

1. Everything is in a constant of motion, producing constant change.
2. Hardship often creates opportunities for shifts, growth, and expansion.
3. Grief is real and should be respected, acknowledged, and honored.
4. Everything in life is fluid, so remember this too shall pass.
5. Avoiding the grieving process increases suffering and elongates the healing process.
6. Utilize "what if" to shift your thoughts and energy.

7. There's a master-divine plan.
8. Lean into acceptance, faith, and trust.
9. You always have a choice, though sometimes it's only how you choose to handle challenges.
10. Leverage the law of least resistance to change the current.
11. Contrast provides clarity of preferences across all areas of your life.
12. Gratitude is an inclusive energy.
13. Look for the gift in your painful or challenging life experiences to shift your vibration.
14. Smiling, helping others, upbeat music, and movies all work to provide space needed to uplift your vibration, and therefore what you're attracting.
15. Remember, tomorrow is a new day.

CHAPTER 12
THE INTERSECTION MATTERS

*"You are very powerful, provided you
know how powerful you are."*
–Yogi Bhajan

The intersection of science and metaphysics is the sweet spot of the Universe. It's where all of your life experiences spring forth, and where you are your most powerful self!

This book presents many new concepts, all of which have been carefully captured in the key principles section at the end of each chapter. To confirm you haven't missed any, they're all consolidated here because: While independently each has the potential to change your life, together they have the power to *transform* it!

Use the following checklist to ensure you've mined all of the gold. Leverage those that resonate and leave behind those that don't:

CHAPTER 1: SCIENCE MATTERS

1. _____Basic science:
   a. All matter is comprised of atoms.
   b. Atoms are pure energy in a constant state of vibration.
   c. Vibrations produce wavelengths and frequencies.
   d. Wavelengths and vibrational frequencies create electromagnetic waves.

    e. High frequencies have waves with quicker intervals.

    f. Low frequencies haves waves with slower intervals.

2.   _____Electromagnetic waves contain information specific to the matter exuding it.

3.   _____The frequency highway encompasses the globe, picking up and carrying information emitted by matter.

4.   _____The frequency highway is the Universe's Search Engine functioning like a browser, picking up emissions, searching for and returning matches.

5.   _____These principles apply to all matter, inanimate or not.

CHAPTER 2: ENERGY MATTERS

6.   _____You are pure energy.

7.   _____Firing neurons create electromagnetic waves known as thought packets that emanate outwards.

8.   _____The Universe's Search Engine searches for vibrational matches to the frequency of your thoughts.

9.   _____The Universe's Search Engine returns real-life experiences based on what you have thought about.

10.   _____You are responsible for your thoughts.

11.   _____Thought vibratory frequencies vary according to what you are thinking.

12.   _____Your thoughts are finite with each thought precluding another thought.

13.   _____Feelings and your mood are indicators of what you're thinking about.

14.   _____Feelings bundle onto thoughts, increasing trajectory and bringing forth matches sooner.

15.   _____The first step in becoming a deliberate creator is determining what you want.

16. _____Use self-awareness to observe and manage your thoughts.
17. _____You're already a master creator.
18. _____Bundled thought transmission is your superpower.

CHAPTER 3: QUANTUM PHYSICS MATTERS

19. _____The frequency highway facilitates the Law of Attraction.
20. _____The Universe's Search Engine is responsible for bringing your life experiences based on matches to your thought transmissions.
21. _____Everything in the Universe has its own vibrational frequency, including your thoughts.
22. _____Frequencies work to harmonize through a process known as entrainment.
23. _____The law of least resistance relates to electrons choosing the path of least resistance.
24. _____Pivot negative frequencies to positive through awareness, then asking what you can do to change the situation.
25. _____Pay attention to feelings as your guidance system indicating the frequencies you are emitting.
26. _____The invisibility of these forces does not preclude their existence.

CHAPTER 4: MANIFESTATION MATTERS

27. _____Manifestation requires a vibrational match to the vibratory frequency of what you desire.
28. _____There is a trap door where all desires that have *not* manifested reside. It's held shut by a worn piece of tape that is ready to break free.

29. _____Living in the space of already accomplishing your desire emits a powerful bundled thought that moves you into manifestation quicker.

30. _____During visualization motor neurons fire up as if you were performing the action.

31. _____Visualization primes the frequency highway for the delivery of your desires.

32. _____Vibrational frequencies are things that can be sent, received, and absorbed.

33. _____Your thought emissions have the power to impact things.

34. _____Your brain has transmitter and receiver functionality, able to emit and receive simultaneously.

35. _____Intention setting is a force of nature, acting like a razor sharp tip on the arrow of your command.

36. _____To increase the power of your intentions have others hold them for you.

37. _____The life you have today is directly correlated to the thoughts you had in the past.

38. _____Not accepting your life situation introduces static and returns more of your current life situation.

39. _____Make peace with your current life situation by finding the perfection of now.

40. _____Your first step in deliberate creation is defining what you desire.

41. _____What can be attracted to you could be better than you can imagine so leave room for the divergence.

42. _____Belief systems are thoughts that have become stuck, blocking your ability to see things as they truly are.

43. _____Self-fulfilling prophecies are caused by belief systems and related emissions.

CHAPTER 5: THE UNIVERSE'S SEARCH ENGINE

44. _____Buried within string particle that makes up the fabric of the cosmos is computer code matching code that drives search engines.

45. _____The Universe's Search Engine simply processes your thoughts as orders.

46. _____The Universe's Search Engine is completely neutral. It doesn't care how kind, mean, deserving or desperate you are.

47. _____The Universe's Search Engine is perfectly perfect at its job, never failing to find and bring you a match, and make you right.

CHAPTER 6: SELF-AWARENESS MATTERS

48. _____Becoming a co-creator requires awareness of the thoughts you emanate.

49. _____95% of your thoughts are subconscious.

50. _____Self-awareness is a muscle that must be worked on, cultivated, and grown.

51. _____Mindfulness and meditation are self-awareness tools.

52. _____When you're exuding thoughts 100% of the time, there's no space to observe and receive.

53. _____Monkey mind is normal.

54. _____Your goal isn't to silence all thoughts, but to tame them over time so you're no longer a slave to them.

55. _____Becoming a deliberate co-creator requires investment of your time, but in the long run less effort is required and the payoff is a happier life.

56. _____It takes more than five positive statements to erase one negative thought.

57. _____Creating space shines a light on your self-talk.

CHAPTER 7: MIND MATTERS

58. _____When you watch someone do something mirror neurons fire as if *you* were doing it.

59. _____Anything you watch processes as your own thoughts.

60. _____The Universe's Search Engine cannot distinguish where a thought originates and takes your emissions as your commands.

61. _____There are no lucky people, only people with an expectation that things always go their way.

62. _____Feelings are a direct indicator of your thoughts.

63. _____Negative emotions are gifts alerting you to your thoughts, motivating you to make changes, and helping you to get clear on preferences.

64. _____Self-worth and value must come from your own value system that is made up of what's important to you.

65. _____Repetitive thoughts reshape your brain making it easier to think those same thoughts.

66. _____90% of your thoughts are the same from the day before, therefore returning 90% of the same experiences and giving the appearance that nothing's ever changing.

67. _____Shift negative vibes associated with heartache, regret, disappointment, failure, grudges and resentment by considering and identifying the lessons.

68. _____Affirmations are powerful tools in rerouting neural pathways and changing limiting beliefs.

CHAPTER 8: METAPHYSICS MATTERS

69. _____Metaphysics is the concern or interest in things other than the material and physical.

70. _____Almost everyone believes in something greater than themselves.

71. _____You are a soul manifesting in physical form.

72. _____Your soul has experiences, knowledge, and wisdom from all lifetimes and is a powerful source of intelligence.

73. _____Interconnectedness is being connected to all things in the Universe.

74. _____Intuition is an automatic sense that when tapped provides guidance and better decision-making.

75. _____Your inner being and intuition are one and the same.

76. _____Your whole soul consists of your incarnated self and your inner being.

77. _____Your inner being is the larger part of who you are.

78. _____Your inner being is connected to Source.

79. _____Connection to your inner being is your natural state of being.

80. _____Foster a relationship with your intuition by asking, "What can I do for you today?"

81. _____Initial thoughts, ideas and memories are initiated by your inner being.

82. _____Foster a relationship with your intuition by asking, "What can I do for you today?"

83. _____Guides are assigned to you throughout your lifetime, watching over and providing guidance.

84. _____Connection to spirit energies is a superpower.

CHAPTER 9: BODY MATTERS

85. _____You live in a material world in a human form with a strong interconnectedness between the soul and body.

86. _____Your body is a tool facilitating your ability to live life on this planet.

87. _____Awareness that you are not your external presence, but rather pure energy inhabiting a physical body, is the secret to enlightenment.

88. _____Move from self-judgment into self-loving.

89. _____Your body is intelligent, so check in and offer gratitude for the work it performs and the experiences it affords.

90. _____View your body as your cherished partner, offering kindness and compassion.

91. _____Don't take your human senses for granted as they are not carried into spirit form.

92. _____Your thoughts also emanate throughout your body.

93. _____There's a heart-mind connection so it's important to listen to your heart to make better decisions.

94. _____Giving yourself and your body credit and gratitude does not a narcissist make!

95. _____The diamond rule is to love yourself.

96. _____It takes more than five positive statements to erase one negative thought.

CHAPTER 10: PURPOSE MATTERS

97. _____Disharmony with your inner being is felt as unhappiness and a dis-ease that can manifest as a disease or illness.

98. _____Your purpose is to live in joy.

99. _____There's nothing you need to do to prove your worth.

100. _____It isn't by accident that you're here; room was made just for you.

101. _____Negative feelings instigate awareness and change

102. _____Happiness is your natural state of being and you deserve to be happy

103. _____Following the breadcrumbs of what brings you joy will always lead you to your purpose

104. _____Your purpose is fluid. As you achieve one another follows. Remain open and flexible in following your bliss

105. _____Get unstuck by bringing the joy.
106. _____Always offer loving compassion to yourself through life phases that make living in joy challenging.

CHAPTER 11: COPING MATTERS

107. _____Everything is in a constant of motion producing constant change.
108. _____Hardship often creates opportunities for shifts, growth, and expansion.
109. _____Grief is real and should be respected, acknowledged and honored.
110. _____Everything in life is fluid, so remember this too shall pass.
111. _____Avoiding the grieving process increases suffering and elongates the healing process.
112. _____Utilize "what if" to shift thoughts and energy.
113. _____There's a master-divine plan.
114. _____Lean into acceptance, faith and trust.
115. _____You always have a choice while sometimes it's only how you choose to handle challenges
116. _____Leverage the law of least resistance to change the current.
117. _____Contrast provides clarity of preferences across all areas of your life.
118. _____Gratitude is an inclusive energy.
119. _____Look for the gift in your stretch assignment to shift your vibration.
120. _____Smiling, helping others, upbeat music, and movies work to provide the space needed to uplift your vibration, and therefore what you're attracting.
121. _____Remember, tomorrow is a new day.

Learning these universal laws and principles can't help but change the way you see, approach and experience life forevermore. There's no way to un-ring the bell.

Investment Needed

From increased health, wealth, joy, love, and whatever matters the most to you, as a deliberate creator if you dream it, you can achieve it by tuning into metaphysical powers and harnessing the power of your thoughts to control what the Universe's Search Engine returns.

Like anything of value, becoming a deliberate creator requires an investment of time, energy and diligence. If you haven't done so already, define what's important to you and create an intention to focus there, keeping the main thing the main thing. Cultivate self-awareness and be devoted to keeping your airways clean, emitting positive, high vibration thoughts.

It's Your Move

The opportunity before you is to create your future reality, becoming the maestro of the orchestra that is this lifetime. Recognizing that the controller has always been in the palm of your hand, it's your move.

I wish you endless love and harmony throughout all of your days. Stay tuned, loving you, and happy searching!

Part Three

The Workbook in Part Three follows the Epilogue. If you've completed the exercises as they appeared, don't miss the Bonus Exercise on page 165 and the Online Challenges on page 167 that come free with the purchase of this book.

EPILOGUE: APPLICATION

Engrained patterns of behavior and thought are what hold us back from becoming a match to our desired state. Because breaking away from these worn in grooves is challenging at a minimum, I've developed trademarked trainings specialized in helping individuals and companies get further faster in creating their future realities and achieving their goals.

FOR ME

You now know that it's possible to create your future reality by harnessing the power of your thoughts to control what the Universe's Search Engine returns.

Knowing is one thing, but the challenge becomes *applying* what you've learned because it requires changing up worn in grooves. Those deep patterns of behavior and thought make changing things up difficult, so a systematic approach is best to expedite your evolution and to improve your circumstances.

That's why I created my trademarked Digital Evolve Courses. You can register for these courses online at anitamscott.com/Courses. The Level 1: Discovery course is yours free with the purchase of this book!

Level 1: Discovery

The Evolve Discovery Course™ is a simple three-step track designed to jumpstart your evolution.

- Step 1: By reading this book you already completed the first step on the journey, learning how to harness the power of the Universe's Search Engine to return your best life.
- Step 2: Take the Evolve Quiz™ to measure comprehension across the universal principles presented to you in this book that are responsible for the entirety of your quality of life.
- Step 3: Complete the Evolve Challenges™ to reinforce concepts and build muscle memory to sustain a happier, healthier, and more successful you.

Level 2: Mastery

For those wanting to gain mastery of the Universe's Search Engine so they can begin experiencing improvements sooner rather than later, the Evolve Master Course™ is the vehicle you're looking for. This online digital course puts you in the driver seat as a deliberate creator within *6 weeks*!

The course curriculum, plan and tools are your blueprint, with step-by-step activities that get you further faster by reducing resistance, deprogramming negative patterns of thought, increasing neuroplasticity, and building new, healthier neuropathways.

The Evolve Master Course™ jumpstarts your future reality so like others before you, well before the course ends you experience amazing transformation and dramatic improvements to your circumstances. This program is an exercise regimen for your mind, and a makeover for your life!

FOR BUSINESSES

With the rapid pace of innovation, all workplace environments must evolve or be left behind. For organizations paying attention, the next great frontier in optimization isn't just Artificial Intelligence. It's also optimizing the workforce through evolved thought consciousness to achieve goals faster, and with more engaged, fulfilled employees.

Just as meditation and mindfulness moved into the mainstream with companies like Google, Goldman Sachs, General Mills, Ford, Nike and Apple offering mindfulness programs to employees once the benefits were scientifically proven, similarly with science proving brain power can be optimized the next step in an organizations evolutionary journey is optimizing the thought consciousness of their workforce.

You know, now, *how* it's possible to create your future reality by harnessing the power of thoughts to control what the Universe's Search Engine returns. This opportunity exists at an organization level too, where companies can harness the power of 'evolved thought consciousness' and the 'collective workforce' to create and realize the organization's desired realty, sooner, with greater success. Imagine the exponential power that businesses access when they optimize an entire workforce, where employees are on the same page with the same intentions, driving towards the very same vision and goals.

While companies focus on upgrading employee's soft skills like emotional intelligence and hard skills across the latest technology advances, leading edge organizations create a strong competitive advantage when they unlock and harness the power of an employee workforce that collectively pools evolved thought consciousness.

To learn more visit: https://anitamscott.com/business

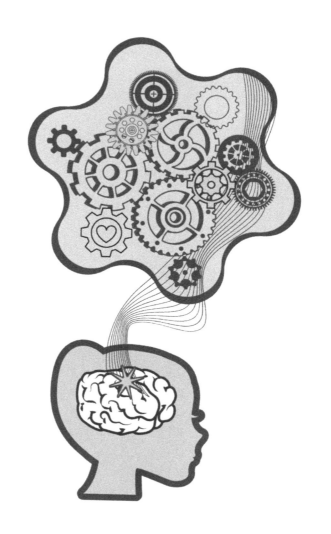

PART III:
WORKBOOK

This workbook facilitates and expedites your evolution by reinforcing concepts and fostering the creation of new neural pathways propelling you towards living your best life.

Exercise 1: Define What You Want

The first step in becoming a deliberate creator is figuring out what's important to you, what makes you happy, and what you want out of life.

Exercise instructions: Complete steps in order.
Time allocation: 30 minutes
Online: https://anitamscott.com/ex1— Password (case sensitive): desire

STEP 1: Take a few minutes to imagine living your best life, with success and abundance in everything that's important to you across wealth, health, love, career, etc.

STEP 2: In the table write anything and everything you want.

Help: Imagine you only have a couple of years to live and all the money in the world. What would you do? What would you want to achieve? What would you buy? What does your dream future look like?

STEP 3: Pump up your wishes by applying: Dream. Dream bigger. Is that all you got?

Help: Rather than taking a one-week vacation to Bora Bora, blow it up to taking a first class, all-expenses paid two-week trip to Bora Bora.

STEP 4: Prioritize according to what you desire from *most to least*

STEP 2: Write down anything and everything you want in life	STEP 3: Dream big. Dream Bigger. Is that all you got?	STEP 4: Prioritize

STEP 5: Finish by taking a mental picture of your highest priority desires. This is where you want to spend more time on focused thinking. The main thing is to keep the main thing the main thing.[36]

EXERCISE 2: RAISE YOUR FREQUENCY

Use the power of appreciation to shift your focus away from what's bothering you, and raise your vibratory frequency so high vibration experiences boomerang back to you.

Exercise instructions: Complete steps in any order.
Time allocation: 20 minutes
Online: https://anitamscott.com/ex2 — Password (case sensitive): raise

STEP 1: Enter the two relationships you enjoy most, and why.

STEP 2: Write top two body parts you appreciate the most, and why.

STEP 3: Enter two activities that make you feel most alive.

STEP 4: Write your two top blessings, strengths and/or natural gifts.

STEP 5: Acknowledge yourself by entering your top two achievements over the past couple of years.

STEP 6: Capture anything else you're grateful for.

STEP 1: Top 2 relationships & why they're your favorite	
STEP 2: Top 2 body parts & why they're your favorite	
STEP 3: Top 2 activities that make you feel most alive	
STEP 4: Top 2 blessings, strengths or natural talents	
STEP 5: Top 2 achievements or learnings over the past couple years	
STEP 6: Anything else you're grateful for	

Going forward, institute a daily practice of writing down what you're grateful for. By doing so you're emanating high vibe thoughts, and harnessing the power of the Universes Search Engine to return positive life experiences.

EXERCISE 3: CHALLENGE BELIEF SYSTEMS

This exercise uncovers belief systems. Once uncovered you have the ability to dissolve any impeding your ability to live your best life.

Exercise instructions: Complete steps in order.
Time allocation: 25 minutes
Online: https://anitamscott.com/ex3 — Password (case sensitive): dissolve

STEP 1: In the table provided write your *beliefs* and *life rules*.

Help: *Believing* in heaven and hell and *believing* you must be saved/ good to get into heaven; if you're bad you'll go to hell.

STEP 2: For each line write "Yes" where **not** having that belief or rule would change your life for the better, and "No" for those that wouldn't.

Help: Ask and answer: What if this wasn't true? How could I live my life differently?

STEP 3: For those with a "Yes" write a sentence or two about how dissolving that belief would improve your life.

Help: How would you be able to live your life differently if this wasn't your truth?

STEP 1: Write your beliefs and life rules	STEP 2: Write 'Yes' if not believing this would improve your life, write 'No' if it wouldn't	STEP 3: For those with a 'Yes' write a sentence or two about how dissolving that belief would improve your life

EXERCISE 4: EXTREME VISION BOARDING

A vision board is a document that has pictures of the things you wish to experience and have in your life. Each time you see your vision board you perform short visualization exercises. Visualization is one of the most powerful mind exercises because it broadcasts and primes the frequency highway to bring the essence of those images into your reality.

It's easier than ever to create vision boards online, up-leveling them to extreme since you're able to locate imagery perfectly depicting your dream life.

Exercise instructions: Complete steps in order.
Requirement: A computer with Microsoft PowerPoint and online access to Google images.
Time allocation: 1 hour
Online: https://anitamscott.com/ex3 — Password (case sensitive): vision

STEP 1: Review and leverage responses from Exercise 1: Define What You Want.

STEP 2: Go online to Google and search for images depicting exactly what you want to experience. Then copy and paste the pictures into an electronic document. Include more or larger pictures for higher priority items to ensure paramount visibility.

Help:

1. Open PowerPoint and create a new file (click "File" then "New").
2. Go to Google and search for images of your top priority (i.e., picture of new house).
3. Click on "Images for…" at top of page.
4. Scroll to find the perfect images.

5. Click on the image (you'll get a bigger version).
6. Right click on the bigger image and select "Copy image."
7. Go back into your PowerPoint and paste the image (Ctrl V or right click & paste).
8. Continue steps 2-8 until all desired images are in the PowerPoint.
9. Format as you like.
10. Save (click "File" then "Save As" and note where you're saving so you can access later).

STEP 3: Print and display your vision board in a prominent place where you can see it every day so you're doing short visualization exercises often. Getting it laminated costs less than five dollars and it looks really nice. Better yet, turn your vision board into your screen saver so you see it multiple times a day.

STEP 4: Before going to sleep at night reimagine viewing the images from your vision board.

EXERCISE 5: THOUGHT DIAGNOSTIC

Given the direct correlation thoughts have to your health and bringing about the circumstances of your life, it's important to perform a diagnostic of them. Since 95% of your thoughts are subconscious (Parton), this exercise helps uncover what you've been broadcasting.

Exercise instructions: Complete steps in order.
Time allocation: 1 hour
Online: https://anitamscott.com/ex5 — Password (case sensitive): thought

STEP 1: Reflect back to a typical day this week and capture everything you did.

STEP 2: Enter how many minutes each activity took.

STEP 3: Mark an 'X' for any rote time, then next to it write down how many minutes of rote in that activity.

Help: Rote is the use of memory with little intelligence (Merriam-Webster). When you're on the highway and don't remember how a car got in front of you, you were in rote. It's when your brain is on autopilot which occurs when performing repetitive activities like driving, doing the dishes, taking a shower and brushing your teeth.

STEP 4: Go deep to recall and capture what you were thinking about during each activity.

STEP 5: Note if the thoughts were of the past, present or future.

STEP 6: Note the emotions you experienced along with those thoughts.

STEP 7: Identify if the emotions were positive (felt good) or negative (felt bad).

EXERCISE 5: THOUGHT DIAGNOSTIC							
STEP 1: Reflect back to a typical day this week and write down everything you did	STEP 2: Write how many minutes each activity took	STEP 3: Mark an X where there is rote time, then capture how many minutes spent in that rote time		STEP 4: Go deep and recall what you were thinking about during each activity	STEP 5: Note if the thoughts were of the past, present or future	STEP 6: What emotions did you experience along with those thoughts?	STEP 7: Identify if positive or negative emotions NOTE: Scroll to bottom for steps 8-11
Activity	Mins	Indicate Rote time with X	Quantify Rote Time in minutes	What Were You Thinking?	Past Present Future	Emotion	Positive Negative
Example: Brush teeth	2	X	2	I'm dreading the presentation	Future	Fear	Negative
STEP 8: Total the minutes:		STEP 9: Total rote time		STEP 10: Present: Future:		STEP 11: Total Positive: Total Negative:	

STEP 8 and 9: In the last row total minutes of activity and rote time.

STEP 10: Total *how many* thoughts were of the past, present, and future.

STEP 11: Total *how many* thoughts were positive, and how many were negative.

When completed, notice how often you think thoughts about the past and future versus the present, and negative versus positive thoughts. The output is your benchmark (starting place). Your goal is to increase present-time thinking and increase positive thoughts. Also notice how much time you spend in rote. Rote is a gold mine of time you can tap into to become more conscious of what you are thinking, and more deliberate about what you choose to think about.

Remember, since what you focus on expands you are unquestionably the most powerful person in your life.

EXERCISE 6: CATCH AND RELEASE

Continually reliving the past means you've created grooves in your brain (neuropathways) that cause you to gravitate towards those memories. When this occurs you keep attracting the same things over and over again so your life experiences cannot improve.

Completing this exercise frees you from those engrained patterns by fostering new neural pathway that move you away from your conditioned, programmed, reoccurring thoughts to higher frequency ones.

Exercise instructions: Complete steps in order.
Time allocation: 25 minutes
Online: https://anitamscott.com/ex6 — Password (case sensitive): release

STEP 1: Write down painful memories you continually think about.

Help: Capture negative memories you relive like a breakup or divorce, loss of promotion, losing a loved one, etc. It could be heartache, regret, disappointment, failure, or something you're carrying like a grudge or resentment.

STEP 2: Next consider and identify the lessons.

Help: What did you learn? How did it change you? What do you do differently because of it?

STEP 1: Write down memories that you continually think about.	STEP 2: Identify the learnings and write them down.

Going forward, when these memories show up acknowledge and thank them by saying, "Yes, I remember that." Then immediately shift your focus to the gifts captured in column two, continuing, "And I'm grateful that I learned …(*what I don't want ever again, my preferences so I have better clarity on what I do want*)." Then choose to move to another, more pleasant thought.

EXERCISE 7: PERCEPTION SHIFTER

Completing this exercise expands your perspective, giving you the ability to view scenarios from another lens.

Exercise instructions: Complete the steps in order.
Time allocation: 30 minutes
Online: https://anitamscott.com/ex7 — Password (case sensitive): shift

STEP 1: Begin by recalling a situation that you didn't handle very well or didn't go your way, and then write a synopsis.

STEP 2: Capture your reaction.

STEP 3: Enter the name of someone you admire and respect, like a role model.

STEP 4: Imagine your role model encountering the same situation and picture how they would have handled it. Write that down.

STEP 1: Recount & write down a synopsis of a situation that you believe you didn't handle very well	
STEP 2: Recount & write down what your response was in that situation	
STEP 3: Think of someone you admire, like a role model, and write their name	
STEP 4: Picture how your role model would have handled this situation, and write that down	

Your opportunity is to up-level how you see things, becoming aware that any situation can be seen through a variety of viewpoints. Choose the lens of least resistance, and give others the benefit of the doubt.

EXERCISE 8: FOCUS SHIFTER

Completing this exercise is helpful when you're experiencing hardship. It forces you to acknowledge that not everything in your life is going wrong, making it easier to pivot your attention to more positive thoughts.

Exercise instructions: Populate each space with something you value and are grateful for across the categories in any order. Use one space for each family member (i.e. Ben), and for those attending school use one space for each class (i.e. Science).

Time allocation: 25 minutes

Online: https://anitamscott.com/ex8 — Password (case sensitive): focus

Family & Friends	Education	Work-Career	Hobbies	Skills	Self	Other

The beauty of this grid is in turning to it when things go wrong, or you lose them altogether. When that happens, shift your focus to the other boxes, acknowledge what you still have that is going well, and be grateful for them. Keep your focus on these positive aspects for as long as possible. This practice shortens the duration of suffering, pushing you through the vacuum of the loss quicker and increasing your vibration at the same time.

BONUS EXERCISE: THE UNIVERSE'S TO-DO LIST

Feeling overwhelmed? This bonus exercise offers relief, while helping you practice the art of allowing and leaning into divine trust by giving your to-dos to the Universe.

Exercise instructions: Complete steps in order, using one box for each to-do.
Time allocation: 20 minutes
Online: https://anitamscott.com/bonus1 — Password (case sensitive): done

STEP 1: Enter everything you need to do today, this week, this month, and this year.

STEP 2: Split those activities across:

A. Your To-Do List: Move anything from column one to this column that's easy or you feel like doing.

B. The Universe's To-Do List: Move everything remaining to this column.

STEP 3: Enter the desired completion date.

STEP 1: Enter all your to-do's, both short-term (needs to get done this week) and long-term (needs to be done over the next few weeks or months)	STEP 2: Review the list of activities for any that feel easy for you to do, then add them to Your To-Do List. Move all the others to the Universe's To-Do List.		STEP 3: Enter desired completion date
	Your To-Do List	The Universe's To-Do List	

As you harness the power of the Universe across science and metaphysics your to-do list becomes shorter and shorter. Ideally, you only take action when inspired to do so, leaving all the rest to be divinely orchestrated.

EVOLVE CHALLENGES™

With the purchase of this book you have access to four *free* online challenges designed to reinforce the concepts covered in *The Universe is Your Search Engine* over a four-week period. Taking this approach helps keep lessons and applications top of mind, supports the development of new and adapted neural pathways, and builds muscle memory which takes between two to four weeks.[37]

Exercise instructions: Complete only one challenge per week to build muscle memory.
Time allocation: 15-20 minutes per challenge

Each challenge consists of three short modules with a three question anonymous quiz at the end to validate comprehension. Use the direct links and passwords below to unlock each challenge.

I. **Week 1: Universe's Search Engine**
   a. Modules: Science, Energy, and Quantum Physics Matters
   b. Link: https://anitamscott.com/challenge1
   c. Password for all three modules (*case sensitive*): expand

II. **Week 2: Get Your Mind Right**
   a. Modules: Universe's Search Engine, Self-Awareness, and Mind Matters
   b. Link: https://anitamscott.com/challenge2
   c. Password for all three modules (*case sensitive*): mind

III. **Week 3: Get Connected**
   a. Modules: Metaphysics, Body, and Your Purpose Matters
   b. Link: https://anitamscott.com/challenge3
   c. Password for all three modules (*case sensitive*): connect

IV. **Week 4: Bonus Challenge**
   a. Modules: Your BFF, Dissolve Your BS, Coping Matters
   b. Link: https://anitamscott.com/bonus
   c. Password for all three modules (*case sensitive*): bonus

GLOSSARY

1. **Affirmations**: Affirmations are positive declarations that you repeat to reprogram your brain, remove limiting belief systems, and improve self-confidence. They have the power to restructure your brain by interrupting patterns and bypassing the worn-in grooves made by repetitive negative thoughts, replacing them with new, healthier neural pathways.
2. **Atoms**: The basic building blocks of matter.
3. **Belief Systems:** Belief systems are programs usually passed down from parents and authority figures that made the world make sense to you, influencing heavily how you operate within the world.
4. **Boomerang Effect:** Bundled thoughts have a more forceful trajectory and therefore travel deeper and faster into the Universe's Search Engine, *returning matches quicker.*
5. **Conscious Passiveness:** While the word "passive" tends to have a negative connotation, in this context choosing to be passive is a Jedi mind trick where you no longer resist and instead, consciously move into trusting that the situation will resolve in its own time and manner with acceptance of whatever the outcome. In this way it is possible to do nothing and accomplish more.
6. **Detractors:** Detractors bundle onto thoughts, slowing down their trajectory and minimizing manifestations. Examples of detractors are dissatisfaction with now, ambiguity of desires, and limiting belief systems.

7. **Divine perfection:** Divine perfection is the concept that there are no mistakes, and that at every moment of every day, everything is as it should be.

8. **Empathetic and mirror neurons:** As you watch someone else do something empathetic and mirror neurons are triggered and light up as if you are performing the actions you see, or as if the activity is happening to you.

9. **Entrainment:** Frequencies working to harmonize because the natural state of being is in harmony.

10. **Evolved thought consciousness:** Leveraging the power of thought and laws of physics to create your future reality.

11. **Feelings:** Your thoughts interconnect with your feelings and can be used as a guidance system alerting you to what you're thinking about, and therefore emanating.

12. **Feeling Bundles:** Interconnected to thoughts, feelings function as intensifiers that bundle onto thought packets strengthening their signals enabling them to travel *faster* and *deeper* into the Universe's Search Engine.

13. **Frequency:** The frequency is determined by how quickly the wavelength completes a cycle of motion every second.

14. **Frequency highway:** The energy field that acts as a conduit bringing together matching frequencies.

15. **Gestation:** The period of time between a desire or thought and the manifestation of it.

16. **Information (Emissions):** Electromagnetic waves emanating from matter.

17. **Inner being:** The whole you includes you in this carnation and your inner being, which is the larger part of you. Together you are the wholly you.

18. **Intentions:** Intention setting is a force of nature, so when you intend something it is far more likely to come to bear. Intentions. An intention is a goal, plan or decision. Intentions bundle onto thought packets acting like an arrowhead with a razor sharp tip coated with a special sauce that is irresistible to the Universe to conspire and bring it to you.

19. **Intensifiers:** Intensifiers bundle onto thoughts, increasing their trajectory onto and across the Universe's Search Engine rendering matches sooner. Examples of intensifiers are feelings, desires, actions, intentions, speaking, having fun, and using visualization.
20. **Intuition:** An instinctual extrasensory perception known as a sixth sense.
21. **Law of Attraction:** The magnetic power of the universe that draws similar energies together.
22. **Law of Least Resistance:** Related to nature where electrons always choose the path of least resistance.
23. **Law of Vibration:** If you were to break down anything to its purest form and analyze it you would find pure energy resonating as a vibratory frequency. Everything in the Universe has its own distinct vibrational frequency.
24. **Life Experiences:** Occurrences in your everyday life that, when strung together, make up your life.
25. **Life plan**: The plan your soul intended before incarnating into this lifetime.
26. **Matter**: Everything with physical substance is called matter.
27. **Meditation**: Meditation is a technique intended to rest the mind, and is used to create space, clarity and grow self-awareness.
28. **Mindfulness:** Being mindful is a mental state where you are fully present, living in the moment, tuned into your thoughts and how you feel on an emotional and physical level.
29. **Motion**: When matter vibrates it is in a constant state of motion.
30. **Motor Neurons**: When you take physical action, motor neurons at the front of your brain fire up and trigger nerve impulses that create your body's movement.
31. **Rote**: Rote is when your brain is on autopilot.
32. **Selective Ignorance:** Being deliberate about what you chose not to devote any time to.
33. **Self-fulfilling prophecy:** A prediction made by you that you inadvertently cause to come true.
34. **Soul**: Your life force that is eternal, and inhabits your body.

35. **Metaphysical**: The concern or interest in things other than material and physical.
36. **Spiritual amnesia:** A veil of forgetfulness from who you were in past lives to make it easier to fully integrate into this lifetime.
37. **Static**: Interference with thoughts due to friction (unhappiness) with the what-is-ness of now.
38. **Stretch Assignments:** Stretch assignments are projects that employees are given outside of their day-to-day job that are designed to give people desiring career advancement an opportunity to learn, grow, and prove themselves.
39. **Subatomic Particles:** Atoms contain pure energy with millions of subatomic particles running around, popping with energy.
40. **Superpower #1:** Bundled thought transmission onto the Universe's Search Engine.
41. **Superpower #2**: Your ability to connect to your inner being and spirit energies.
42. **Universe's Search Engine:** The frequency highway that brings together matching frequencies, also called energies.
43. **Vibrations**: All that energy popping around creates constant vibrations.
44. **Vibratory Frequencies:** Different thoughts produce unique vibrational frequencies that range from high (stemming from positive thoughts and feelings like love, joy, gratitude) to low (stemming from negative thoughts and feelings like jealousy, revenge and hate).
45. **Visualization**: Imagining something or picturing images in your mind.
46. **Wavelength**: A wave's length is the distance between the two peaks or two valleys of the electromagnetic wave.

BIBLIOGRAPHY

1   Joki, A. (2018, November 25). *Does the human brain emit any electromagnetic waves, or they are only called brainwaves because of the firing pattern of the neurons?* Retrieved September 10, 2019, from Quora: https://www.quora.com/Does-the-human-brain-emit-any-electromagnetic-waves-or-they-are-only-called-brainwaves-because-of-the-firing-pattern-of-the-neurons

2   Sasson, R. (n.d.). *How Many Thoughts Does Your Mind Think in One Hour?* Retrieved January 19, 2019, from Success Consciousness: https://www.successconsciousness.com/blog/inner-peace/how-many-thoughts-does-your-mind-think-in-one-hour/

3   Cromack, C. (2014, January 2). *Is it possible to have more than one thought at a time?* Retrieved Januray 20, 2019, from Quora: https://www.quora.com/Is-it-possible-to-have-more-than-one-thought-at-a-time

4   Hicks, E. (2019, July 13). Daily Quote – July 13, 2019. San Diego, CA, USA.

5   Comedy Central. (2018). *Jokes - The Lottery Ticket.* Retrieved January 18, 2019, from Comedy Cenral Jokes: http://jokes.cc.com/funny-god/1gkcpp/the-lottery-ticket

6   Schmalbruch, S. (2015, January 28). *Here's The Trick Olympic Athletes Use To Achieve Their Goals.* Retrieved January 14, 2019, from Business Insider: https://www.businessinsider.com/olympic-athletes-and-power-of-visualization-2015-1

7   Emoto, D. (2009, March 13). *Water, Consciousness & Intent: Dr. Masaru Emoto.* Retrieved January 18, 2019, from YouTube: https://www.youtube.com/watch?v=tAvzsjcBtx8

8   Mctaggart, L. (2009). *THE INTENTION EXPERIMENT, The Germination Intention Experiments.* Retrieved January 18, 2019, from lynnemctaggart.com: https://lynnemctaggart.com/wp-content/uploads/2016/09/germination-experiment.pdf

9   Jean Larson, P. C. (n.d.). *How Does Nature Impact Our Wellbeing?* Retrieved April 3, 2019, from Taking Charge of Your Well Being: https://www.takingcharge.csh.umn.edu/how-does-nature-impact-our-wellbeing

10 (2015). *Quantum Physicist: Consciousness Arises Outside of the Brain* Retrieved December 3, 2019, from Whitley Strieber's UnknownCountry.com: http://www.unknowncountry.com/news/quantum-physicist-consciousness-arises-outside-brain

11 Jr., D. J. (2015, March 26). *Theoretical Physicist Finds Computer Code in String Theory.* Retrieved 14 2019, January, from You Tube: https://www.youtube.com/watch?v=cvMlUepVgbA

12 Freud, S. (2019). *IZ Quotes.* Retrieved April 12, 2019, from IZ Quotes: https://izquotes.com/quotes-pictures/quote-the-mind-is-like-an-iceberg-it-floats-with-one-seventh-of-its-bulk-above-water-sigmund-freud-66024.jpg

13 Szegedy-Maszak, M. (n.d.). *Mysteries of the mind: Your unconscious is making your everyday decisions.* Retrieved January 18, 2019, from Auburn University: http://www.auburn.edu/~mitrege/ENGL2210/USNWR-mind.html

14 McLeod, S. (2015). *Unconscious Mind.* Retrieved January 25, 2019, from Simply Psychology: https://www.simplypsychology.org/unconscious-mind.html

15 Ph.D., E. M. (2013, September 11). *20 Scientific Reasons to Start Meditating Today.* Retrieved January 14, 2019, from Psychology Today: https://www.psychologytoday.com/blog/feeling-it/201309/20-scientific-reasons-start-meditating-today

16 Gallagher, B. (2011, November 3). *Buddha: How to Tame Your Monkey Mind.* Retrieved January 14, 2019, from Hiffington Post: http://www.huffingtonpost.com/bj-gallagher/buddha-how-to-tame-your-m_b_945793.html

17 Parton, S. (n.d.). *The Science of Happiness: Why complaining is literally killing you.* Retrieved January 21, 2019, from Psych Pedia: https://psychpedia.blogspot.com/2015/11/the-science-of-happiness-why.html

18 Ramachandran, V. (2009). *The neurons that shaped civilization.* Retrieved January 18, 2019, from TedIndia: https://www.ted.com/talks/vs_ramachandran_the_neurons_that_shaped_civilization

19 Burns, W. (2016, April 28). *How Understanding Luck Will Improve Your Organization's Creativity.* Retrieved January 18, 2019, from Forbes: https://www.forbes.com/sites/willburns/2016/04/28/how-understanding-luck-will-improve-your-organizations-creativity/#7eeec6a6546b

20 Stillman, J. (2016, February 29). *Complaining Is Terrible for You, According to Science.* Retrieved February 29, 2016, from Inc.: https://www.inc.com/jessica-stillman/complaining-rewires-your-brain-for-negativity-science-says.html

21 Chopra, D. (2014, May 13). *Soul of healing meditations.* Retrieved January 18, 2019, from YouTube: https://www.youtube.com/watch?v=-xzP2c4FQr4

22 Merriam-Webster.com *Did You Know?* feature (n.d.). *Metaphysics.* Retrieved January 19, 2019, from Merriam-Webster Dictonary: https://www.merriam-webster.com/dictionary/metaphysics

23 Wilding, M. (2018, March 8). *How to Make Better Decisions by Improving Your Intuition.* Retrieved January 18, 2019, from Better Humans: https://betterhumans.coach.me/how-to-make-better-decisions-by-improving-your-intuition-a5ede405d7af

24 Freud, S. (2019). *IZ Quotes.* Retrieved April 12, 2019, from IZ Quotes: https://izquotes.com/quotes-pictures/quote-the-mind-is-like-an-iceberg-it-floats-with-one-seventh-of-its-bulk-above-water-sigmund-freud-66024.jpg

25 Moses. (1450 - 1410 B.C., July 12). *Bible, Old Testament. Genesis 6:4.* Grand Rapids: Zondervan.

26 HeartMath, LLC. (2017, December 6). *Let Your Heart Talk to Your Brain.* Retrieved January 19, 2019, from Huffington Post: https://www.huffpost.com/entry/heart-wisdom_b_2615857

27 Matthew. (1450 - 1410 B.C., July 12). *Bible, New Testament. Matthew 22:39.* Grand Rapids: Zondervan.

28 Jack Zenger, J. F. (2013, March 15). *The Ideal Praise-to-Criticism Ratio.* Retrieved January 19, 2019, from Harvard Business Review: https://hbr.org/2013/03/the-ideal-praise-to-criticism

29 MacLeod, A. (2009). The Instruction, Living the Life You Intended. Boulder CO: Sounds True.

30 Job. (1450 - 1410 B.C.). *Bible, Old Testament. Job 1-3.* Grand Rapids: Zondervan.

31 2019 IAC Publishing, LLC. (n.d.). *What Is Sigmund Freud's Iceberg Theory?* Retrieved 4 14, 19, from Referece*: https://www.reference.com/world-view/sigmund-freud-s-iceberg-theory-befcbf1fb28c1d50

32 Moses. (1450 - 1410 B.C., July 12). *Bible, Old Testament. Genesis 6:4.* Grand Rapids: Zondervan.

33 Unknown. (n.d.). *The Story of the Chinese Farmer.* Retrieved January 14, 2019, from YouTube: https://www.youtube.com/watch?v=OX0OARBqBp0

34 Beckwith, M. (2017, February 6). *Activate Your Potential.* Retrieved January 14, 2019, from YouTube: https://www.youtube.com/watch?v=uBeE3maoI4s&t=340s

35 Ronald E Riggio Ph.D. (2012, June 25). *There's Magic In Your Smile.* Retrieved March 3, 2019, from Psychology Today: https://www.psychologytoday.com/us/blog/cutting-edge-leadership/201206/there-s-magic-in-your-smile

36 Covey, S. (n.d.). Retrieved March 24, 2019, from Brainy Quotes: https://www.brainyquote.com/quotes/stephen_covey_110198

37 Blaise Collins, P. (2018, Decemeber 9). Retrieved January 14, 2019, from Quora: https://www.quora.com/profile/Blaise-Collins-PhD

CPSIA information can be obtained
at www.ICGtesting.com
Printed in the USA
LVHW011551210720
661234LV00004B/541

9 781982 240066